GW00818480

AND DISTRICT

VOLUME 15

compiled by

Dr. Haldane Mitchell

A Rotary contribution to local history

Dedicated to all the fine artistes who performed at the Book Launches over the years.

(Club Chartered 30th June, 1955)

Published by the Rotary Club of Omagh
c/o Kevlin Lodge
40 Ballynahatty Road
Omagh
Co. Tyrone BT78 1PW

November 2007

ISBN: 0-9541891-3-2
      978-0-9541891-3-6

© Copyright reserved.

Whilst all care has been taken in compiling this book,
the Publishers cannot be held responsible for any inaccuracies in the text.

All rights reserved under international copyright conventions.
No part of this publication may be reproduced or utilised in any form or by any means, electronic or mechanical, including photocopying, recording or by any information, storage and retrieval system without the prior permission in writing from the Publisher.

Designed and printed at
Grahams Printers Ltd., Omagh, Co. Tyrone

Front cover:
Strule Arts Centre
(opened 8th June, 2007)

Back Cover:
Montage showing
Strule Arts Centre, Omagh College
and the Sacred Heart Chapel

FOREWORD

by **Richard Collins**

President of Rotary Club of Omagh 2007 / 2008

*L*ooking back at the previous volumes of "Images of Omagh and District", it is hard to quantify the sheer volume of historical information they contain. Needless-to-say, they have been a true and honest portrait of the life and passage of time in our town and district.

This volume contains remembrance and reflection of a wide variety of places and people who have shaped the character of the community we live in and is a further reminder that any society is a sum of all its parts, great and small, as well as good and bad.

It contains timely reminders for the upcoming generations that the reality of a full life will, in all probability, see periods of peace and periods of conflict. It is all too easy to forget the personal endeavours, sacrifices and tragedies experienced by the past and existing generations of Omagh. Therefore, it is important and fitting to remember them — all of them!

On behalf of the Rotary Club of Omagh, we sincerely thank our fellow member, Dr. Haldane Mitchell, for his innovation and dedication in producing these wonderful series of books.

ACKNOWLEDGEMENTS

*T*he Council and Members of the Rotary Club of Omagh would like to acknowledge the contributions of the following to Volume 15 of "Images of Omagh and District".

Norman Anderson Collection, Father Donal Gillespie, William Anderson *(R)*, Angus Mitchell (Photographer), John Hall, Marie O'Neill, Patrick McLoone, Monteith Collection, Michael and Aileen Pollard, Noel Mitchell, Frank Chesney, Tom McDevitte *(D)*, Brian McDaid, Mark McGrath, D.O.E. Roads Service (Omagh), Photography of Carmel Gillespie and Bridie Meyler, Omagh Probus Club, Ed Winters Photography, Robert and Betty Smith, Austin Lynch (Director, Ulster Herald Newspapers), Brian Johnston, W. D. Fyffe, Tyrone Constitution, Jackie Sloan (Photographer), Omagh Library, Alan Neil (Photographer), Ulster-American Folk Park, Desmond and Valerie Graham, The Staff of Grahams Printers Ltd., Frank Sweeney (Dept. of Arts and Tourism, (ODC), Omagh District Council, Omagh Motor Club, West Tyrone Historical Society, Father Kevin Mullan, P.P., Carmel and Danny McGrath, Elaine and Dai Waterson, Catherine Johnston, Sam Connor (Photographer), Jim and Una Hunt, Lily Stewart *(D)*, George Hamilton *(R)*, Campbell Henderson, Sam and Eileen Hammond, George Stewart *(R)*, Michael Gaine *(R)*, Gerald and Rita Devlin, Captain R. Ellis *(R)*, Sylvia and Michael Hart, Edward Scott *(R)*, John Johnston, Torney Collection, Kenneth Crane Collection, Wesley Atchison *(R)*, Tyrone Constitution, Jack McMillin *(D)*, The Academy (Omagh), Tom Davidson, Marion Mitchell, Eithne McClelland, Pat McSorley (Photographer), Patrick Chesters, John McCandless, "North West Ulster" by Alistair Rowan, "The Gate Lodges of Ulster" by J. A. K. Dean, Henry Cooper, Ivan Brown, Geoffrey Simpson (Viewback Auctions), Arthur O. Quinn, Norman Holland Collection, Paddy Moore *(D)*, Valerie White *(D)*, Gary Milligan, Raymond and Lee Anderson, Marshall Fenton, William McGrew, Tyrone Farming Society, Harry McCartney, Omagh Academicals Rugby Football Club, John Chambers, May Wiltshire, Deirdre Dunphy, Marcus Piggott *(D)*, Isobel Anderson, Rubena Campbell, Tyrone County Club, Kathleen Hinds, Tom Sweeney, Jackie McGale, Uel Henderson, John Lyons, Dorothy Hastings, Gregory Parke *(R)*, Richard Collins *(R)*, Royal British Legion, Daryl Simpson, Western Health and Social Services Board, Sylvia Graham, James Beattie, Helen Gilmour, Ulster-American Folk Park, John Bradley, Jean Thompson, Patricia Colman, Maud Steele, Mina and Robert Wilson, Terry Patterson, Rev. Leslie Casement (Sixmilecross Presbyterian Church), Isobel Palmer, Norman Cochrane, Sammy Armstrong *(D)*, Eva Donaghy *(D)*, Bernadette Grant, Valerie McKee, Gertie McCauley, David Crawford (Railway Photographs of Irvinestown, Kesh, Pettigo, Castlecaldwell, Belleek and Ballyshannon — Copyright Charles P. Friel Collection), Tom and Bobby McFarland, Kenneth Collins, Marie Slane, Eileen McElroy, Mary McCullough, Chris Passmore, Kate Law.

(R) denotes Rotarian
(D) denotes Deceased

CONTENTS

CHAPTER 1

Ordnance Survey Memoirs
Statistical Report
by **Lieutenant William Lancey** Royal Engineers (7th March, (1834)

NATURAL STATE *Locality and Extent*

The Parish of Drumragh <Drumreagh> is situated in the County Tyrone, Barony of Omagh and Diocese of Derry. It is surrounded by the parishes of Ardstraw, Cappagh, Clogherny, Donacavy, Dromore and East Longfield and contains 20,160 acres.

NATURAL FEATURES *Hills*

This parish is, for the most part, a low country of round hills called "drums" with raths or forts on their summits from whence its name of Drumrath is derived. Towards East Longfield it attains at Corridinna the height of 972 feet, but this is the only mountain in the parish. The greater part is under cultivation, and the soil is far preferable to that of the adjacent parishes.

Greetings from Omagh.

Ordnance Survey Memoirs

General Appearance

The general appearance of Drumragh indicates superior wealth, industry and good management. Having the advantages of good land and a ready market, there is every encouragement for an outlay of money. Much has been done of late years, but fencing, ditching and draining are still a good deal neglected. The parish taken collectively is in a more civilised state than those adjoining it.

Rivers and Lakes

Two small streams called the Owenreagh and Quiggery unite above the old church and take the name of the Drumragh River which at Omagh mingles with the Camowen <Cammon> which divides this parish from Cappagh.

The Fairy Water bounds a portion of the north of Drumragh. It is celebrated for fine pearls, some of which are scarcely inferior to those of the East. They are found in fresh water mussels <muscles> which abound in the streams round Omagh. Pearls in the summer season can always be obtained in Omagh and are not confined to the Fairy Water. The Drumragh, Camowen and Strule <Strewel> produce them and some of the best are found in Mountjoy forest. They can be purchased for a trifle: the finest, about the size of a pea, for 4 or 5 shillings.

The Abbey Bridge built around 1900.

Lakes

[Insert addition: There are 4 lakes situated in Lough Muck, Firreagh, Kivlin and Rylands. The two former are the principal, that of Lough Muck being the largest, and contains [blank] acres. It is prettily situated and famous for pike, eels and perch. That at Fireagh is also celebrated for pike. A boat on Lough Muck is a great attraction to the people of Omagh. It belongs to Mr. Campbell].

MODERN TOPOGRAPHY *Buildings in Omagh*

The principal buildings in Drumragh are [in] the county town of Omagh, in which are included the court house of assize, gaol, infirmary, the church, 2 meeting houses, Methodist chapel <chaple> Roman Catholic chapel and barracks.

Court House

The court house stands on the hill at the head of the main street. It is a handsome plain building of cut freestone, with a Doric portico of 4 columns with a pediment. It contains a large vestibule opening into Crown and Civil Courts, retiring rooms for the judge and juries, a large room for the grand jury and a handsome dining and drawing room for their accommodation, with a kitchen and lock-up place for prisoners on the underground floor. The Crown Court has 2 galleries for the accommodation of the public and one for the grand jury, whose official room opens into it. The civil court is small, without a gallery, and

The Assizes around 1903.

has little space appropriated to the people. This building was erected on the site of the old gaol in 1814. The portico was added in 1820 and the whole cost by county presentments, 17,000 pounds. The freestone for its erection was obtained from West Longfield and the columns from Mulnatoosnog in Drumragh.

Gaol

The county gaol stands at the west end of the town on the Derry road. It consists of the old and new gaols. The former was built in 1796 of common stone and is now used as the women's and debtors' prison. The new part was erected in 1823 of cut freestone in a semicircular form, divided into [blank] wards, each having a separate yard for the different classes of prisoner. Both old and new gaols are 3-storeys high. In front of the old building an open space has lately been enclosed for the prisoners to work in, and the whole building is surrounded with a high stone wall to prevent their escape.

This establishment can accommodate 300 prisoners and is guarded by 14 keepers. The numbers for trial in 1829 were 113, in 1830 172, in 1831 144, in 1832 93, in 1833 137, total tried 659. Of these none suffered the extreme penalty of the law. 34 were transported for life, 5 for 14 years and 94 for 7 years, amounting to 133 transports.

High Street before the days of the motor car.

The governor's house stands in the centre of the arc formed by the new gaol and looks into each yard. His salary has lately been reduced to 150 pounds a year. The keepers receive gaol <goal> allowance and 1s 6d a day wages.

The tread mill is of small dimensions and its power is only applied to raise water for the building from a deep well adjacent to it.

SOCIAL ECONOMY *Police*

There is a lock-up house in the new market, a police barrack over the bridge and one close to the church for the internal peace of the town. 2 officers of the constabulary are stationed in Omagh.

Infirmary

The county infirmary, situated in the town, is a building of small extent for such a purpose. It is supported by a grant from government of 100 pounds Irish, by county presentments and by private subscriptions. The number of patients for 1833 was 234. The prevailing diseases are scrofula, lues, veneria, ulcers and accidents. The surgeon's salary is 120 pounds Irish and the annual expenditure between 700 and 800 pounds per annum. It would be well if this building were sold and one better suited to the purpose erected in the country.

Dispensary

The dispensary is supported by presentments and private subscriptions. The number relieved last year were 1,217, at an expense of 90 pounds.

High Street after the building of the Monument in 1904.

The surgeon's salary is 50 pounds and the usual diseases fevers, dyspepsia and pectoral complaints.

MODERN TOPOGRAPHY *Places of Worship: Church*

The parish church, situated in the town, is very inconveniently placed for the greater part of the parish. It is a neat building with a high spire. It was built about 100 years ago and the spire added in 1810. In 1818 a new roof was put on the church and in 1827 it was enlarged at an expense of 145 pounds and second commodious gallery added. It can contain 1,000 people and in the summer any festival is generally well filled. Since 1792 the sum of 1,300 pounds has been assessed on the parish for the repairs of the church.

Presbyterian Meeting Houses

There are 2 Presbyterian places of worship: one called the old meeting house, with 3 half galleries, stands on the Dublin road. It was built in 1717 and cost 800 pounds. It had a thatched roof replaced by a slated one about 10 years ago, and was fully repaired in 1830.

The new meeting house without galleries cost 600 pounds and stands on the road to Dromore. The first Presbyterian congregation, worshipping in the old house, are accommodated to the amount of 800 persons, the second congregation in the new house to the amount of 372. In the summer they are generally full. The new house was built by subscription in 1754 and was

Trinity, the Sacred Heart and St. Columbas.

repaired and ceiled in 1830 at an expense of 62 pounds. The stipend of the minister is 30 pounds with 50 regium donum added. The stipend of the minister of the first congregation is 60 pounds, with 100 pounds regium donum.

Methodist Chapel

This place of worship is a neat building. [It] has a gallery and is nearly opposite the church. It was built in 1812 and pays 5 pounds a year ground rent. It is pewed and well fitted out and can contain 250 people. It is usually well filled by persons of various denominations, the number of Methodist families not exceeding 60. There is a good house attached for the resident preacher. Omagh and Newtownstewart are in the same circuit.

Roman Catholic Chapel

The Roman Catholic chapel in Brook Street is a modern building erected in 1829, the former place of worship being on the Derry road beyond the barracks. It cost 700 pounds and can contain 1,500 persons, having a gallery on 3 of its sides.

Barracks

The barracks at Gortmore is divided from the gaol by a narrow lane. It was an ordnance barrack for 1 troop of horse artillery, for which there was every convenience for officers, men, horses and guns. It is now occupied by a detachment of infantry, consisting of 2 officers and 44 rank and file, a

The Sacred Heart Church and Bell's Bridge.

detachment of 1 officer and 26 men being stationed at Lifford. Infantry to the amount of 8 officers, 110 rank and file and 60 horses could, if necessary, be quartered in this barrack at present. There are also quarters for a barrack-master and sergeant, officers' mess-room, hospital, engine house and a good well.

Town of Omagh

The county town of Tyrone consist[s] of 1 main street with 4 avenues leading to the adjacent bridges. It is situated on the left bank of the Camowen River, 86 miles from Dublin and 26 from Derry. The centre of the town, in which the church and court house are situated, stands on a hill, which is a great inconvenience to travellers. There are several good private houses and numerous good mercantile establishments, with 2 hotels who let post horses. Jaunting cars can also be hired from 2 other houses at cheaper rates than at the hotels.

The daily public conveyances are the Derry and Dublin mail up and down, a chaise marine to and from Derry and a mail car to and from Gortin. A day coach from the White Hart runs to Dublin every Monday, Wednesday and Friday, and returns the alternate days. An opposition coach from Derry to Dublin runs the same days as the Omagh coach. [Insert marginal note: a chaisemarine leaves Omagh for Enniskillen on Monday, Wednesday and Friday and returns the following days].

High Street in the 1950s.

SOCIAL AND PRODUCTIVE ECONOMY *Markets*

A weekly market is held on Saturday, every alternate week being a large market and every first Saturday in the month a fair. The cloth market is held every fortnight opposite the White Hart Inn, the corn and potato markets in Brook Street and the new market near Bridge Lane. Meal and butter are also sold in this square. The sheep markets are in front of the infirmary and at the corner of Church Street. Pigs are sold in the open space near the court house and the last mentioned sheep market. The cattle market is between the church and the new Presbyterian meeting house, and the horse fair at the Dublin end of the town. There are meat shambles of an inferior kind, but on market days it is exposed for sale in the public streets. the markets are all good and families can have all their wants supplied. Beef sells at 3d ha'penny a pound, mutton at 4d, butter at 7d ha'penny, bread, a 4 lb. loaf for 12d.

Proprietors

The principal proprietors of the town are General Archdale of Fermanagh, who has the ground rent but only 2 tenements. The houses chiefly belong to Mrs. Spiller, John and George Buchanan, James Greer and the orphans Hamilton, the heirs of Alexander Campbell and John and Samuel Galbraith. The inhabitants are estimated at 2,400 one-half of whom are Protestants. Many have attained to independence. They dress and live well. Some of them are moral and some few religious.

Market Street in the 1950s.

Schools

There are good schools for all ranks of the inhabitants. The curate educates 40 boys in classics at the rate of 30 guineas a year for boarders, and 8, 6 and 4 guineas for day scholars. This school is of immense advantage to the town as the respectable merchants can educate their children well, under their own eyes, at a cheap rate.

Respectable female children are instructed by Mrs. Duncan, who has 16 day scholars at the rate of 8 guineas per annum, music and drawing included, with a separate charge for the French language.

Miss McArthur's preparatory school for male and female children contains 36 scholars at 4 guineas a year; Mr. Alcrow's school 36 male children, English and arithmetic for 4 guineas per annum.

The church free school supported by the rector educated 80 male and 40 female scholars, principally Roman Catholics. The master receives 13 pounds a year, assessed at parish vestry annually, and does not reside in the house, which stands at the church door.

A London Hibernian school under the management of Mrs. Spiller is built at her garden gate. There are 40 scholars. The society grants 4 pounds and she pays the rest of the expenses, amounting to about 16 pounds per annum. The mistress resides and on the Lord's Day assists in instructing 60 scholars.

A busy High Street in the 1960s.

MODERN TOPOGRAPHY *Country Places of Worship*

The principal buildings not in town are the Seceders' houses in Gillygooley and Ballynahatty and Drumragh Roman Catholic chapel in Firreagh.

The Gillygooley house is fully pewed, that at Ballynahatty is partly pewed. Neither has galleries, and they would hold about 150 persons each. The minister receives 50 pounds bounty and 20 pounds stipend and performs service in each house every other Sunday.

Drumragh chapel is the old parish place of worship for the Roman Catholics. It is partly thatched and partly slated. It has 1 gallery and will hold about 900 persons.

Rectory and Newgrove

The rectory at Tattreagh Glebe and Newgrove, the residence of Samuel Galbraith Esquire. The rectory was built by Dr. Richard Stack about 25 years ago and cost 2,000 pounds, 100 of which was paid by the Board of First Fruits. It is a commodious house with every requisite for a person of wealth.

Newgrove has been lately enlarged and the demesne comprising 100 acres much improved.

Village of Ballynahatty

The only village is that of Ballynahatty, a small place of no importance. Audley Mervyn, its ancient proprietor, had it in contemplation to build the town there, after the destruction of Omagh by fire in 1743.

Campsie before the motor car.

Dwellings

There are many very respectable houses belonging to the better class of farmers, and the buildings generally in this parish are of a superior description to those of the immediate vicinity. The cabins are thatched and usually white-washed.

ANCIENT TOPOGRAPHY *Monastery*

The site of the old monastery is shown at the pound near the dry bridge in Omagh, said to have been built in the 14th century by the O'Neill family and in modern times occupied by Audley Mervyn, who was the proprietor of Omagh and a large territory around it. The ruins of this monastery, converted into a castle, were in existence 50 years ago, but were taken down to obtain stones for rebuilding the town, which had been accidently burned on the 4th May 1743. This castle was an extensive pile of building, but now no vestige remains of it.

Castle and Fort

Audley Mervyn also had a large castle at Ballynahatty, the site of which is still known, the remaining stones having been removed to erect a modern house within these few years. A garrison of King James' troops held in Omagh from January to July 1689. A fort at that time stood on the elevated ground near the present site of the court house. This garrison fled from the town before the forces of King William.

Campsie Bridge in the 1950s.

Old Church

Drumragh old church is pleasantly situated on the river of that name, and has the walls and gables yet standing. No account can be obtained respecting its history, except that it was burned in Cromwell's time, rebuilt and is now a ruin.

Old Bell

An old bell about 9 inches long was dug up by the ancestors of a family called McAnkill in the neighbourhood of the graveyard. It has been handed down to the present generation and is always rung for the corpses of their family when on the road to and at the place of interment <internment>. They state that two of their ancestors in company with a third person, on leaving the burial place, heard the ringing of this bell under their feet, but the ears of the third were holden. On turning up the ground they found the bell, which will not sound for any but one of the McAnkills. It is kept by the oldest of the race and always rings the morning of the approaching death of any of the family. The lord of the soil took the bell, but as he could not get it to ring he returned it to the McAnkills. This family claims descent from that of St. Columbkill and are of the Roman Catholic faith.

Chapel

Near the fort called the Mass House Hill Fort, at the back of Mr. Rodger's house in Cavanacaw, a Roman Catholic chapel was erected 100 years ago by a famous priest named Father Terence McCawell. This chapel was afterwards taken down and removed to Mulloughmore and subsequently erected in Firreagh, its present situation.

Killyclogher Chapel and School. The Chapel was built in 1820.

Holy Wells

There is a well in Mullaghmenagh called Tubberdoney, said of old to be good for sore eyes. It is now unfrequented. There is also a well at Cornabracken, where the people dip their sick children at Midsummer's Eve, and one at Tattykeel above the mill where they wash themselves for ulcers. These are only frequented by the Roman Catholics.

Forts and Giant's Grave

There are many forts in Drumragh, one in Drumconnelly with 3 parapets and 2 ditches. Others have single ditches: a large one of this kind is behind Mr. Rodger's house in Cavanacaw, and a very commanding one at Beagh, one at Loughmuck, one at Makeeragh, one in Gillygooley, one in Tullynenry, one in Tattyreagh Glebe and many others whose situations will be seen on the plans. There are no legends respecting them, except the usual one attributing their erection to the Danes. Attempts have been made to discover gold in these forts, but whether they have been attended with success it is difficult to say; but I have been informed by respectable authority that Mr. Watson of Mallaghmenagh dug out of the fort on his land silver coins of an ounce weight which he disposed of.

A giant's grave stands on the mearing of Cornabracken and Deerpark and one in Loughmuck.

High Street in the 1950s with the Town Hall on the left showing the underground toilets.
They were destroyed by a bomb in 1974.

SOCIAL ECONOMY *Landlords*

There are no resident landlords except Mr. Samuel Galbraith of Newgrove, George Buchanan of Tattykeel and Mr. Rodgers of Cavanacaw. Others possessing property in Drumragh reside near the parish, and much of the land has the benefit of the personal inspection of those who derive their wealth from its inhabitants: Lord Belmore of Castlecoole, Sir James Stronge of Tynan Hall, Sir Hugh Stewart of Ballygawley, Sir James Bruce of Downhill, Reverend Hamilton Stewart of Buncrana, Reverend Lowery of Somerset, Lieutenant-General Hamilton of London, Mervyn Stewart Esquire of Ballygawley, John Galbraith Esquire of Greenmount, Sir John Burgoyne of Strabane, Mrs. Spiller of Omagh, Alexander Hudson, Esquire of Dublin, Thomas Armstrong of Fellow's Hall, Armagh, with the residents mentioned above are the principal of possessors of the soil.

Inhabitants

Many of the inhabitants not living in the town are wealthy and independent. They are industrious, civil and anxious to improve. There is generally work for the poor, and absolute poverty might here be almost unknown. About one-half are Roman Catholics, who generally comprise the poorer classes. Few migrate for harvest either to England and Scotland.

Schools

Besides the schools mentioned in connection with the town of Omagh, there is one at Corlea having 66 male and 44 female children, the master residing

Tyrone County Hospital opened in 1899.

near the house; one at Tattykeel, 25 males and 22 females, master resides. Drumragh school has 36 males and 21 females, master and mistress reside; Sir James Bruce gives them 5 pounds annually and an acre of land. Cavanacaw, 80 males and 54 females, master resides amongst the scholars. Gillygooley, 52 males, 48 females, master resides. Dressog school (lately maliciously burnt down); Ballynahatty private school, 30 males and females (Latin taught) and Tattykeel private school for Latin and English, 20 boys. The society scholars pay 6s a year and the Latin pupils 2 pounds. The Protestants and Catholics go to the same teachers and no school under the new National Board has yet been opened in Drumragh.

Dispensary
The dispensary in the town of Omagh already described supplies the medical wants of the poor of this parish.

PRODUCTIVE ECONOMY *Farms Rent and Tenure*
The size of farms varies from 5 to 60 acres, the average being 25 acres. Any land less than 5 acres is generally held by the labourer under the large farmer, and the rent paid either by work or money as agreed on. The average rent of good arable land varies from 3 half guineas to 30s down. It is held for 3 lives or 31 years, or 2 lives and 21 years, bishop's land as usual for 21 years and some is renewable for ever. General Hamilton's estate is an old lease now depending on an aged life, and lets for 13s an acre. This property returns to the proprietor only 350 pounds, which sum will be doubled at least on the death of the above life. There is no grazing farm in Drumragh and very little

The Lovers' Retreat, acquired by the Urban Council from the Stack Estate.

mountain for the farmers' young cattle. Some of the farms are kept in excellent order. Amongst the best are those of Joseph Moore on Sir James Bruce's estate and Mr. Osborn's on Lord Belmore's property.

Crops

The usual rotation of crops is first potatoes, then oats, barley, flax, forced grass and wheat. Mr. Moore crops his land with oats, the potatoes, wheat or barley, flax and grass seed, hay and 2 years grazing. Iron ploughs are very general

Manures

The chief manures are lime mixed with farmyard manure. The lime is purchased at Kilmore quarry at the rate of 2s 6d a ton, and that obtained from West Longfield for 5d a cartload for as much as they can draw with 1 horse out of the quarry. It is not unusual for the farmers to draw out much more than they can remove to their farms and leave it on the side of the road for a future opportunity. 1 ton of stone burns into 10 barrels of lime.

There is an old quarry in Mullaghmenagh on General Hamilton's estate, but it is nearly exhausted.

Livestock

Cattle, the old Irish breed, some Ayrshire and some of the Devonshire breed, but the best come from Fermanagh. They sell in the Omagh market from 4 pounds to 7 pounds a head and there is usually a large supply. The farmers raise their own calves, some 10, 8 or 6 head annually.

First Omagh Presbyterian Church, Dublin Road, Omagh — opened in 1897.

Good farm horses with occasionally good roadsters are to be found in Drumragh. The former sell from 10 to 20 pounds, the latter depend on their quality, but there are none of superior breeding. The markets of Enniskillen and Moy are the usual places where good horses are sought for in this neighbourhood.

The best breed of sheep comes from Fermanagh. These when ready for market sometimes sell for 3 pounds a head, the usual price being about 40s. Country sheep vary from 20s to 35s, but as the soil is principally cropped there are few kept in this parish.

Pigs abound at a price varying from a few shillings to 5 pounds; a few of the Dutch breed in the parish.

Fish and Game

Salmon, trout, perch, pike and eels, partridges and snipe are not rare, but hares and woodcock are scarce. A few pheasants are met with at Newgrove and the vicinity of Ballynahatty.

Orchards

There are a few orchards of small extent adjacent to the farmers' or gentlemen's houses. Those of Newgrove and Riverland are the principal. Common fruit is sold in Omagh market at the rate of half a quart for gooseberries and 30 apples for a penny. The chief supply is brought from Loughgall and purchased in the Aughancloy market, and transported by cars and carts to Omagh.

The Leap Bridge showing, from the left, Harvey's scutch mill, the railway bridge and Lisnahoppin House in the background.

Mills

The corn mills are situated in Blacksessagh, Ballynahatty, Edergoole, Loughmuck, Drumshanely, Tattysallagh, Aghydulla, Tattykeel, Dressog, Gillygooley, Coolaghy and Rathnelly. The usual dimensions of the wheels are 10 feet in diameter. Some are undershot, others overshot.

The flax mills are in Blacksessagh, Loughmuck Gillygooley and Coolaghy. Their wheels are less than 10 feet and are adapted to their situations with respect to the fall of the water. The mill at the Omagh brewery is much used by the neighbouring residents of Drumragh.

Manufactures, Prices and Wages

The chief manufacture is linen cloth. About 17,000 webs, 52 yards each, are sold annually in the Omagh market and average 9d ha'penny a yard, which amounts to 34,991 pounds 13s 4d. The trade is declining. The weavers usually earn from 10s to 15s, but some make 24s by 10 days work. This chiefly depends on the quality of the article. The farmers grow their own flax and make their own linen, but journeymen who work for others are the best paid in the linen trade. Grey country cloth is only manufactured to a small extent as it can be purchased cheaper than most farmers can make it. It sells from 2d 6d to 4s 6d a yard. Blankets and flannels are made for country use and bring from 9d to 11d a yard. Stockings are knit in almost every farmhouse and sell from 1s to 2s a pair.

The usual manufacturers of shoes and hats are carried on in Omagh as in other towns. All the common articles of wearing apparel are made for country purposes and every description of English dress can be purchased in the shops. There are 2 tanneries in town which manufacture a good deal of leather. Bricks are made in Ballygowan and sell from 13s to 15s a thousand. The soil is well calculated for this branch of trade and sometimes 100,000 have been made in one season. The price of labour is the same as in Cappagh. Men receive 50s to 63s a half year, women 24s to 30s; daily wages from 8d to 12d a day.

MODERN TOPOGRAPHY *Communications*

The mail road from Dublin to Derry passes through Omagh. It has been alluded to in the statistics of Cappagh. The principal crossroads in Drumragh run to Fintona, Dromore, Ballynahatty and Drumquin; they are all in tolerable repair.

A new line of road from Omagh to Enniskillen passing through Dromore and Irvinestown has lately been opened, which will avoid many of the hills. A chaise marine has been established on it, which leaves Omagh for Enniskillen on Monday, Wednesday and Friday and returns the following days. A conveyance of the kind has been long wanted on this line and no doubt if conducted with care and attention will bring profit to the proprietors and very much accommodate the public.

The country roads are tolerably well kept and there are sufficient of them.

NATURAL FEATURES *Woods and Plantations*
There are few plantations and no woods in the parish. There used to be oak woods in General Hamilton's property in Mullaghmenagh. Gillygooley and Corlea, and that of George Buchanan's at Tattykeel, but they have been all destroyed, some 60, some 30 and some 20 years. Young plantations in Tattykeel, Ballynahatty and Newgrove have lately been put down, but nothing to any extent. Many of the good farmhouses have a few trees about them, which considerably enlivens their appearance.

Fuel
Turf and bog wood are the general fuel of town and country. Scotch coal can be purchased at Strabane, and that from Dungannon is brought to Omagh and sells at 20s a ton. Turf is 5d a box, the same dimensions as that described in Cappagh.

Rocks
The lowlands of Drumragh lie to the south on a strata of clay sandstone, on the north on strata of silicious sandstone, towards the east the lowest strata of mountain limestone are quarried, and the mountain of Corridinna on the west is composed of talcose slate. A basaltic dyke traverses West and East Longfield and is seen in the south west end of Drumragh. The soil is good, of a clayey nature and appears to be highly productive.

SOCIAL ECONOMY *Need for Church and Mills*
A second church is very much wanted: the Protestant population is extensive and many of them remain at home on the Lord's day, pleading their distance from the parish church or the want of sufficient good clothing to appear where the congregation is so well dressed, a very mistaken but very prevailing notion. There is a good site for a church at Riverstown or Mullaghmore on the estate of Samuel Galbraith Esquire, who offered to give 100 pounds and an acre of land if the late Bishop of Derry would allow him to present the curacy during his life. This was refused and the church not built.

Corn and flax mills are much wanted in the neighbourhood of Drumragh. There is a good site for one at the old bridge. The culture of wheat is increasing very much and there being no mills nearer than Dungannon or Strabane, a good wheat mill might not prove a bad speculation near Omagh. [signed] William Lancey, Lieutenant Royal Engineers, 7th March, 1834.

Replies to Queries of the North West Farming Society

NATURAL STATE AND NATURAL FEATURES *Name and Features*
Answer to queries for the information of the North West Society of Ireland.

Section 1. Name, Parish of Drumragh, townlands 52, soil 8,000 acres arable, mountains 2,000 acres, rivers 1, lakes 3, sea coasts none, plantations Newgrove, the seat of Samuel Galbraith Esquire.

Quarries
Section 2. Mines none, minerals none, quarries yes; different kinds of stone, limestone, freestone and building stone.

MODERN TOPOGRAPHY *Buildings*
Section 3. Modern buildings: court house, hospital and gaol. Towns: Omagh, population 1864,. Gentlemen's seats: Samuel Galbraith Esquire, Newgrove, Reverend Robert Burrowes, Riverland. Scenery: hill and vale, skirted with mountain. Inns: 2 principal inns, David Gree's and John Harkin's.

Roads: The country is well intersected with useful and convenient roads.

ANCIENT TOPOGRAPHY *Ancient Buildings*
Section 4. Ancient buildings: 2. Churches: one in the townland of Drumragh, of which there is no history extant. Castles: one, supposed to be built in the year 1400.

Comforts and Health
Section 5. Food: potatoes, meal, milk, butter, beef and mutton and bacon. Fuel: turf. Diseases: none peculiar to this place. Instances of longevity: John O'Neill, late of Omagh, died at the advanced age of 104 years.

Character and Customs of Inhabitants
Section 6. Genius <genious> and disposition of inhabitants: as to genius, though good, nothing very particular. As to disposition, generous, good-natured and most amenable. Language: English. Manners, customs, christenings, marriages, wakes, funerals, traditions: the same as in other parts of Ulster.

Education

Section 7. Education and employment of children reading and assisting in farming and weaving. Schools: 14; collection of books: none; manuscripts: none of such consequence as is thought worthwhile to insert.

Religion

Section 8. State of religious establishment: [blank] Tithes: 530 pounds per annum. Churches 1, meeting houses 4, chapels Roman Catholic 2, chapels Methodist 1.

PRODUCTIVE ECONOMY *Agriculture*

Section 9. Modes of agriculture: [blank]. Rotation of crops: potatoes, barley, flax and oats, whilst the land will bear a crop. Horses: a vast number of horses for agriculture, but few of a good breed. Black cattle: the cows in general are not of a good kind. Pigs in general not of a good kind. Fairs and markets: 11 fairs in the year in Omagh and weekly markets in Ballinahatty. A weekly market in Omagh on Saturday, which is well supplied with linen and every article of provision. Wages and price of labour: from 10d to 1s per day for a labourer [and] horse and [cart] from 4s 2d to 5s per day.

Commerce

Section 10. Trades: carpenters, tailors, weavers, shoemakers, saddlers. Manufactories none, no commerce except by woolen ware, house, groceries' shops and large quantities of brown linen purchased on market days. Navigation none.

SOCIAL ECONOMY *Eminent Men*

Section 11. Natural curiosity none, remarkable occurrence none. Eminent men: the Dean of Cork; writers: the Dean of Cork.

Improvements

Section 12. Suggestions for improvement and means for ameliorating the condition of the poor; no improvement in the agriculture in the parish for upwards of 20 years, except in a very few instances, for want of a good spirited and resident gentry.

CHAPTER 2

The Ulster Volunteer Force
or The War Against Home Rule

WARS AND TROUBLES

Omagh has been a garrison town from possibly the 10th century but history doesn't relate from exactly when. Certainly there was a monastery at Cappagh about this period and a bell from the establishment remains in the National Museum in Dublin similar to the Drumragh-McEnhill Bell that is kept in the Sacred Heart Church in Omagh.

The O'Neills who ruled this area from early times had many castles all round their lands for protection, the oldest still standing as a proud ruin nearest Omagh is Harry Avery's Castle in Newtownstewart built in the 14th century.

The earliest recording of a castle in Omagh is found on the oldest map of the town which is dated 1609 and is kept in the Library of Trinity College in Dublin. The castle stood where the Community House is today with a further fort surrounded by a moat at the top of the town where the Courthouse stands today — nothing remains of either.

In the 15th century a monastery was founded for Franciscans of the Third Order Regular at Gortmore. It remained until the demolition of the monasteries in 1603 when the land was granted to James Mervyn. Nothing remains of the Abbey despite many stories being told of holy wells and tunnels to various places.

Four other monasteries were built for the same order in the region of Newtownstewart and Ardstraw but only the one at Corrick, built on a promontory above the meeting of the Owenkillew and Glenelly rivers, remains as a ruin.

The St. Lucia Barracks on the Derry Road which is thought to be built on the Abbey lands, was built by Colhoun Brothers of Derry and opened in 1881.

The Inniskilling regiments were stationed here as was the regimental museum until the present troubles when British regiments and the Ulster Defence Regiment (U.D.R.) were both stationed together. The regimental museum was transferred to Enniskillen in the 1970s and the U.D.R. was succeeded by the Royal Irish Regiment (R.I.R.) Home Battalions until disbandment and closure of the barracks on the 31st July, 2007.

The Ulster Volunteer Force

Harry Avery's Castle, Newtownstewart.
Named after Henry Ambreidh O'Neill who died in 1392. The castle sits on a magnificent site
overlooking and protecting the Mourne Valley and can be seen for miles around.

Corrick Abbey built around 1465.
The highly picturesque remains of this abbey afford an idea of the original extent and elegance
of the buildings (Alistair Rowan — North West Ulster). The abbey and grounds were granted to
Sir Henry Piers in 1603.

A typical Ulster Volunteer.

UVF

Sir Edward Carson, the man behind the Ulster Volunteer Force.

The Ulster Volunteer Force

Omagh Unit No. 4 U.V.F.

The 2nd Battalion Tyrone Regiment of the U.V.F.
on parade at Crevenagh Holm in 1914.

Wars and Troubles

H Company 2nd Battalion U.V.F., Beragh.

U.V.F. Beragh — Mobile Force 1913 at Clougherny Rectory.

The Ulster Volunteer Force

Baronscourt Camp U.V.F. 1913.
Col. Harry Alexander (ringed) above windscreen of motor on the right of picture.

On parade in front of wash-up facilities at Baronscourt Camp in 1913.

A SHORT HISTORY
The Raising of the Regiments

In 1688 the people of Enniskillen raised Infantry and Dragoon Regiments to defend their town against the forces of the deposed king, James II. So successful were they, that they were incorporated into the army of William III, becoming the 6th Inniskilling Dragoons and the 27th Inniskilling Regiment. Enniskillen is the only town in the British Isles to give its name to two regular regiments.

The 27th Inniskillings

After many campaigns world-wide, the Inniskillings gained a unique honour at St. Lucia in 1796, when their General ordered that their colours be flown from the flagstaff of the captured fortress for an hour, before the hoisting of the Union Flag. They again won undying glory at Waterloo, where they held the centre of Wellington's line in the face of cavalry charges and artillery, only relieved by the charge of the Union Brigade, which included the 6th Inniskilling Dragoons. As the Royal Inniskilling Fusiliers, they will be forever remembered for their undaunted attack against the Boers on Inniskilling Hill, where their doctor won the VC.

In the First World War thirteen battalions of Inniskillings won many further honours with the Irish and Ulster divisions, including eight VCs, the most of any Irish regiment. In the Second World War, after losing many men in the early defeats at Dunkirk and in Burma, the Irish fighting spirit of the Inniskillings was a key to the success of the Irish Brigade in North Africa, Sicily and Italy. Post-war, the Regiment served in small wars in Malaya, Cyprus and Kenya, before amalgamating to form the Royal Irish Rangers in 1968.

The 6th Inniskilling Dragoons

The Inniskilling Dragoons charged at Dettingen and Sherrifmuir, and at Waterloo their gallant and costly charge with the Union Brigade brought essential relief to the beleaguered 27th Inniskillings. An Inniskilling Dragoon now guards Wellington's statue. In the Crimea, the Regiment charged at Balaklava with the Heavy Brigade, defeating a much larger force of Russian cavalry. In the Boer War, they took part in one of the last real cavalry campaigns. In 1912, during Scott's Polar Expedition, Inniskilling Captain Lawrence Oates, suffering from severe frost-bite, walked out to his death rather than impede his comrades. The regiment celebrates his example every St. Patrick's Day.

In the First World War, the Dragoons charged once, but mostly served dismounted. After the war they amalgamated with the 5th Dragoon Guards, who had served with them in the Jacobite Wars and at Balaklava. As the 5th Royal Inniskilling Dragoon Guards they gave up their horses for tanks in 1937, and the Second World War was soon upon them. They fought a skilled withdrawal to Dunkirk in 1940 and returned on D-Day for the victorious sweep across Europe. Post-war, they saw active service in Korea, Aden, Cyprus and Northern Ireland, before amalgamating to form the Royal Dragoon Guards.

Our heritage belongs to all traditions

The Inniskilling Regiments welcomed Irishmen of all traditions into their ranks, where they blended in an atmosphere of equality, friendship, mutual respect and a unique partnership which to this day shows what Irish people working together can achieve.

THE BOER WAR: Ref. Vol. 9 *"Images of Omagh"*

Reverend Robert J. Patterson.
Founder of the Catch-My-Pal
Protestant Total Abstinence Union.

ACROSTIC ON
"Catch=My=Pal Union."

Come Men and Boys do all you can,
At home, abroad, to catch the man
Travelling to destruction.
Catch and bring him, who'er he be,
Hold him right fast, till pledged is he.

Make the effort to bring one more,
You were brought by a brother before.

Prove faithful, don the badge of blue,
All who see it will vote you true ;
Leave nothing undone to gain your end,

United we stand, to help your friend.
Never look back, press onward, and see
Ireland sober, is Ireland free,
Oh work in God's name, blessing hath come,
Now falling in showers on country and home.

"Catch My Pal" dare to be true,
You have a work, no other can do.

Baronscourt, Newtownstewart where the large Catch-My-Pal demonstrations were held in 1910.

Catch-My-Pal demonstration at Baronscourt 1910.

The Rev. Robert J. Patterson
addressing a section of the demonstration at Baronscourt in 1910.

CHAPTER 3

World War I

Archduke Franz Ferdinand and his morganatic wife were assassinated on the 28th June, 1914 in Serajevo the capital of the Balkan province of Bosnia once part of the ancient kingdom of Serbia. This was the catalyst that would eventually start the hostilities of World War I.

When the war started, Ireland was in the middle of the Home Rule crisis with the U.V.F. being formed, armed and drilled to be prepared for all eventualities should they arise in Ulster.

We will never know what the outcome would have been as the majority of the recruits joined up to form the 36th Ulster Division that would end up in the north of France, many at the Somme where over 5,000 Irishmen would die on the first day of hostilities.

St. Lucia Barracks in Omagh became the recruiting centre for the North West and so many men came forward that a temporary camp *(see below)* was set up in what we know as the army holm.

Camp for recruits at Omagh Military Holm.

Departure of 6th Battalion from Omagh Station.

Draft from 3rd and 4th Battalions passing for the Front at Omagh Station.

World War I

The 6th Battalion marching along James Street to Omagh Station.

Colours leaving for the Front in December 1918.
They are passing the G.N.R. goods depot where the Station Centre stands today.
Gallows Hill is in the background.

The lady is checking hay for the horses at the Market Yard Goods Branch where the Omagh Library stands today.

The 9th Battalion passing through Omagh to the camp at Randalstown.

World War I

The Ambulance Train arrives at Omagh Station on 1st May, 1915 on its second visit.

Ref. Vol. 6 *"Images of Omagh"* pages 132 and 133.

An injured soldier being helped off the train en route to the Tyrone County Hospital.

A less injured soldier about to leave the train.

World War I

Scene at the Courthouse celebrating the end of the war.

A group of soldiers at ease outside the Sacred Heart Church before attending Mass.

World War I

*A mixed parade of Military and Royal Ulster Constabulary
going to Trinity Presbyterian Church for the laying up of colours.
This was a custom years after hostilities had ceased.*

The parade entering Trinity Presbyterian Church.

*Aerial view of Strathroy Aerodrome occupied by the Royal Flying Corps
for a period in 1918 up until the end of the war.*

*Following an air crash in November 1918 between Dromore and Trillick — three
pilots were killed (two English and one Canadian).
This is the funeral of the Canadian, called Booth, on 13th November, 1918 passing
Crawford & Wilson's on the High Street on its way to the Dublin Road Cemetery.*

World War I

Royal Flying Corps' sports at Strathroy in the summer of 1918.
Major Joy mounted for the Donkey Derby.

The ladies' egg and spoon race being closely observed by an officer.

World War I

Lieut. W. H. Fyffe at Ballykinlar Training Camp in County Down in 1914.

Lieut. W. H. Fyffe (back right) with some of his comrades at the same training camp.

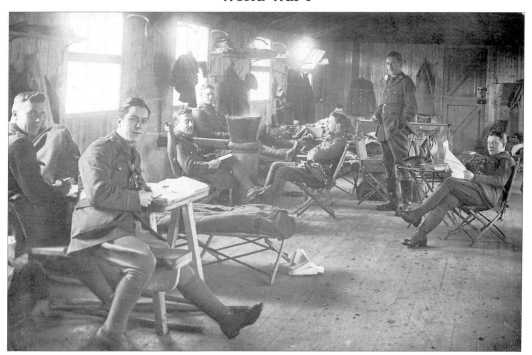

Lieut. W. H. Fyffe, now in the Machine Gun Corps,
moved to Grantham in Lincolnshire for further training.
The photo shows the conditions in the Spider Hut where they lived during training.

A group of Royal Navy personnel in Russia during the First World War.
Second from the right (front row) is Ollie Clements, a brother-in-law of W. H. Fyffe.

THE
PRESBYTERIAN
CHURCH
IN IRELAND,
FIRST OMAGH.

ROLL CALL
SERVICE,

— ON —

SABBATH EVENING,
6TH AUGUST, 1916,
AT 7 O'CLOCK.

CONDUCTED BY
REV. ANDREW MACAFEE,
B.A.

ROLL OF HONOUR

KERR, Nurse Myra, Salonika.

ADAMS, Capt. Alfred, R.A.M.C. Detached
Section No. 2 Mobile Bact. Lab., Salonika.
ALEXANDER, Private Benjamin, R.A.M.C., France. *KIA*
ARMSTRONG, Private Hamilton, R.A.M.C.
Military Hospital, Cork.

BASSETT, Lieut. Edward, 7th Brigade Canadian
Infantry, attached to Headquarters Staff.
BASSETT, Major Jack, Aid-de-Camp to Sir Sam Hughes.

CAMPBELL, Sapper Wm., Royal Engineers, France.
CAMPBELL, Sapper Hugh, Royal Engineers, France.
CAMPBELL, Private John, 2nd Batt. Royal
Inniskilling Fusiliers, France.
CAMPBELL, Private Robert, 38th Batt. Canadian
Infantry, France.
CARSON, Private Robert, 9th Royal Inniskilling Fusiliers.
CARSON, L-Corpl. Wm. John, 9th Royal Inniskilling
Fusiliers, Machine Gun Section, France.
CARSON, Private Samuel, 12th Royal Inniskilling Fusiliers.
CARSON, Private Tom, 12th Royal Inniskilling Fusiliers.
CHAPMAN, Private W.O., R.A.M.C., Dartford War Hospital,
Kent.

ROLL OF HONOUR — continued

CLEMENTS, Charles, E.R.A., H.M.S. Indomitable.
CLEMENTS, Olley, E.R.A., H.M.S. Devonshire.
CLEMENTS, Tom, Cadet, 12th R. Inniskilling Fusiliers, Finner.
COCKBURN, Signaller James, 90th Winnipeg Rifles, France.
COCKBURN, Private Samuel, 90th Winnipeg Rifles, France.
COLQUHOUN, 2nd-Lieut., Hugh, 12th Royal Scotts, France.
COLQUHOUN, Samuel, 7th Batt. Officers' Cadet Corps, Curragh.
COULTER, Private Henderson, 9th R. Inniskilling Fusiliers.
CRUICKSHANK, Capt. Philip, 9th Batt. Royal Inniskilling
Fusiliers, France. *KIA*

DUNCAN, Capt. A. H. R., R.A.M.C., 108th Field Ambulance,
France.

FINNEY, Serg. John, 9th R. Inniskilling Fusiliers, France. *KIA*
FLOOD, 2nd-Lieut. Robert Reginald, K.O.Y.L.I., attached to
Machine Gun Section, France. *KIA*
FLOOD, Private Basil, Canadian Infantry, France. *KIA*
FYFFE, 2nd-Lieut. Wm., 10th South Staffords, England. *KIA*

HUNTER, Serg. Alfred, 3rd Batt. King's Royal Rifles. *KIA*

LOGAN, Trooper Simon, North Irish Horse.
LYNN, Private Robert, 2nd Batt. Canterbury Regiment, New
Zealand Expeditionary Force, France.
LYNN, Private Wm. Thomas, North irish Horse, France.
LYNN, Driver Samuel, Transport Service, 9th Royal
Inniskilling Fusiliers, France.
LYNN, Private James, Royal Engineers, France.
LYNN, Gunner John, Royal Field Artillery.

McCONNELL, 2nd-Lieut. Samuel, 5th Batt., Royal
Inniskilling Fusiliers, Clonmany.
McCONNELL, Private John James, 1st Royal Scotch
Fusiliers, France.
McCONNELL, Private Joseph, 6th Munster Fusiliers,
Machine Gun Section, Salonika.
McCONNELL, Private Samuel, Signal Troop, E.E.F., Upper, Egypt.
McCORMACK, Major R. J., Medical Inspector Affiliated
Hospitals; President of the Standing Medics Board for
Officers; Non-Commissioned Officers and Men; Medical
Supervisor of Recruiting; Embarkation Medical Officer.
McFARLAND, Private William, 1st Batt. Royal Inniskilling
Fusiliers *(Prisoner in Germany).*
McFARLAND, Private William, 168th Company Army
Service Corps, France.
McFARLAND, Private Robert, Royal Irish Rifles, France.
McKIBBIN, Corpl. Hamilton, 4th Batt. Royal Inniskilling
Fusiliers, France.

MAGENNIS, Sergt. Nathaniel, 12th Batt. Royal Inniskilling
Fusiliers, France.
MILES, Sergt. Wm., South African Horse, General Smuts'
Division, East Africa.
MONTGOMERY, Capt. S. A., R.A.M.C., 4th Cavalry Field
Ambulance, 2nd Cavalry Division, France.
MULLAN, St.-Sergt. W. T., M.F.W., R.E., Egypt.

NEELY, Corpl. Jack, North Irish Horse, France.

PATRICK, Private Wm., 3rd Batt. Royal Inniskilling Fusiliers,
France.
POLLOCK, George, Munition Works, Belfast.
POLLOCK, Private James, R.A.M.C., France.

QUIGLEY, Sergt. Andrew, South African Contingent.
QUIGLEY, Private Arthur, Canadian Infantry, France.

SCOTT, 2nd-Lieut. Maddin, 1st Batt. London Scottish, France.
STEVENSON, L.-Corpl. Henry, 12th Batt. Royal Inniskilling
Fusiliers, France. *KIA*

TADLEY, L.-Corpl. John, 12th Batt. Royal Inniskilling
Fusiliers, Finner.
THOMPSON, Telegraphist Ernest, H.M.S. Benbow.

WATSON, Private Robert S., 48th King's Canadian
Highlanders, France. *KIA*
WATSON, Private Robert, 9th Missisangra Horse,
Canadians, France.
WILSON, L.Corpl. Robert, 9th R. Inniskilling Fusiliers, France.
WHITE, Private Joseph, 2nd Batt. Canadian Pioneers, France.
KIA

KIA — Killed in Action

CHAPTER 4

Motoring

When the motor-car came to Omagh it came via two sources. The well-off members of the public who could afford one and the officers who came to St. Lucia Barracks bringing often a more exotic type of vehicle that appealed to the younger man and often of foreign make.

It is said that the officers invited the local gentry to compete with their cars in driving tests on the rough parade ground of the Barracks but the younger officers always won due to their agility and they usually retired to the Mess where the automobile was discussed rather than the driver.

It was not until 1923 that the Omagh Motor Cycle Club was formed following the first running of the Cookstown '100' Motor Cycle Race; the motorists of the town were invited to join the club. This they did but it was not to last and on 1935 the Motor Club was formed and except for the war years it has continued functioning for the competition needs of the motorists in North West Ulster with respect to Rallies, Driving Tests, Hill Climbs and Navigation Classes.

In 1954 the club was given its Certificate of Incorporation and wrote its Constitution. It is now a Limited Company with 35 directors.

An early automobile outside the Officers' Mess at St. Lucia Barracks with a group of officers posing for the photograph.

Motoring
Omagh's Grand Prix Driver
Hugh Charles Hamilton (GB)
18th July, 1905 – 26th August, 1934

Born in Omagh, County Tyrone, Ireland in 1905 and moved to England in 1922. Hamilton started off with motorcycles and reliability events. Started car racing in 1930 with a Riley. Worked as salesman for MG and also raced their cars. He was the top British driver when he in 1934 raced Grand Prix Maseratis for team Whitney Straight and private MG Magnette in Voiturette events. His career came to a sudden end however at the Swiss GP where Hamilton on the last lap slid off the road and into a tree. Hamilton died instantly.

1934: DNF Tripoli GP / DNF Casablanca GP / DNF Mannin Moar / DNS Eifel GP / 5 Montreux GP / DNF Penya Rhin GP / 4 Marne GP / DNF German GP / 2 Albi GP / DNF Coppa Acerbo / 1 Coppa Acerbo (Voiturette) / DNF Swiss GP

From the archives of **Bob Montgomery,** *motoring historian.*

REMEMBERING 'HAMMY': In the Golden Age of 1930s Irish motor racing, one outstanding figure is today little remembered, except by a handful of knowledgeable enthusiasts. Hugh Hamilton deserves better for in the brief five years between 1930 and 1934 he established himself as one of the outstanding drivers of his day.

Born in Omagh in 1905, Hugh Caulfield Hamilton was interested in cars and cycles from an early age. Indeed, when a neighbour acquired an early car, young Hugh, or 'Hammy' as he was more generally known, appeared and offered to wash it. When he was caught driving the car away, his excuse was that he was taking it home to wash it! After his father's death, his mother re-married and the family moved to England.

The pits at the Ards TT Races in the 1930s.

Motoring

Hammy joined University Motors — the MG concessionaires — as a salesman and soon afterwards made his competition debut in 1930 at the wheel of a $4^{1}/2$ litre Bentley when he entered, and won, three races at the Easter Brooklands meeting. He placed third in the 1931 Brooklands Double Twelve Race but it was his fighting drive in the Ards TT Race of that year which made his reputation. Against established stars such as Campari, Birkin and Earl Howe, the Ulsterman placed as high as second before a broken valve rocker ended his race.

The Ards TT Race was perhaps to provide his greatest moment when in 1933 driving an MG he led the great Nuvolari for much of the race until a disastrous pit-stop cost him no less than $7^{1}/4$ minutes and the lead.

An extraordinary fight-back then began and incredibly, Hammy re-took the lead. But on the last lap he was forced to stop for petrol, handing Nuvolari a 20 second lead in the process. Despite Nuvolari also running low on petrol on the last lap the Italian took the victory after six close hours of intense racing.

Opportunities now arose for Hammy to drive in Continental races where he acquitted himself with distinction. In 1934 Hammy made his Grand Prix debut in the Tripoli race driving a Maserati. Once again he demonstrated his

Hugh 'Hammy' Hamilton

outstanding ability, moving up to second place behind Achille Varzi before being side-lined with ignition problems. Over the rest of the season, Hammy took fifth at the Montreux GP and fourth in the Marne GP. At Albi he was second. Turning to the K3 MG, Hammy won at Pescara before heading with his good friend, Dick Seaman, to the Berne GP.

There, on the final lap, Hammy's story came to its end when his Maserati left the road and crashed into a tree. The post-mortem, however, showed that he had suffered heart failure before the accident.

Hammy was buried at Berne where the world's top drivers paid him their last repects. How good was he? It's generally acknowledged that it's impossible to compare drivers across the different eras of racing but I believe that in this case it's safe to say that Hugh Hamilton was perhaps the greatest Irish racing driver of any era.

Memorandum and Articles of Association of
Omagh Motor Club Ltd.

THE COMPANIES' ACTS, (NORTHERN IRELAND)
1932.

Company Limited by Guarantee and not having
a Share Capital.

**Memorandum and Articles
of Association**

OF

OMAGH MOTOR CLUB, LIMITED

No. N.I.3344.

Certificate of Incorporation

I HEREBY CERTIFY that the OMAGH
MOTOR CLUB, LIMITED, is this day
Incorporated under the Companies
Acts (N.I.) 1932, and that the
Company is Limited.

Given under my hand at Belfast,
this Sixth day of April, One Thousand Nine Hundred and Fifty-four.

J. McAllister,

Assist. Registrar of
Companies for Northern
Ireland.

PRELIMINARY

1. Subject as hereinafter provided, the regulations contained in Table C in the First Schedule of the Companies Act (Northern Ireland) 1932 (hereinafter referred to as Table C) shall apply to the Company and, in case of conflict between these articles and the regulations in Table C, the provisions herein contained shall apply.
2. Clauses 2, 11, 29, 32 and 47 of Table C shall not apply to the Company.

MEMBERS

3. The number of members which the Company proposes to be registered is fifty, but the directors may, from time to time, register an increase in members.
4. The Directors shall have power to recommend to the members in General Meeting the election as Honorary Members of persons who have rendered distinguished service to the Club or to the Sport. Such Honorary Members shall have all the privileges of ordinary members, they may vote at a General Meeting or enter the competitions of the Club.

SUBSCRIPTIONS AND ENTRY FEES

5. The Annual Subscriptions of the Club, if any, be fixed at each Annual General Meeting for the ensuing year. For the first year the subscription shall be ten shillings per member.
6. The Directors may, with the sanction of the members in General Meeting, require payment of an Entrance Fee by applicants for membership. The amount of such Entrance Fee and the time and the manner of payment thereof to be determined by the members in General Meeting.

QUORUM

7. No business shall be transacted at any General Meeting unless a quorum of members is present at the time when the meeting proceeds to business; save as herein otherwise provided; five members personally present shall be a quorum.

**NAMES, ADDRESSES
AND DESCRIPTION OF SUBSCRIBERS**

H. G. TORNEY, 12 Campsie Road, Omagh
Garage Proprietor

N. A. DONAGHY, Dublin Road, Omagh
Incorporated Accountant

W. DONNELLAN, 13 Church Street, Omagh
Bank Official

G. H. REILLY, 19 High Street, Omagh
Dental Surgeon

GERALD MURNAGHAN, Birchfield, Omagh
Solicitor

W. BENTHAM WHITE, Benbawn, Omagh
Civil Servant

JOSEPH P. ROBINSON, Innisfree, Gortmore Drive, Omagh
Local Government Officer

WITNESS to above signatures this 22nd day of March, 1954:

J. E. V. McFARLAND, 3 Rodgers Villas, Omagh
School Attendance Officer

Cars owned by the Johnston families
of Rosemount and Mountjoy House in the 1930s.

Mrs. Georgina M. Johnston (née Orr), previously of Correnary (born 1876, died 1957) with her son Herbert at Mountjoy House. Her husband was John Johnston of Killybrack (born 1866, died 1938).

Mabel Johnston of Mountjoy House, married John Ralph McMillin in 1930 (born 1904, died 1975).

From the Minutes of Omagh Motor Club

(1935)

A meeting was advertised and held in Miss Shutes, Market Street, Omagh on Friday, 29th July with the object of forming a Motor Club in Omagh and near District. The following attended: Messrs Taylor, Sharpe, McSorley, McGrath, Owens, Moorehead, Torney, McCabe, Mitchell and Guy.

Mr. McGrath was elected to the chair and the following discussion took place. That a Club should be formed called the Omagh and District Motor Club, the subscription to be 5/s per annum and social and competitive events arranged as soon as possible. The Club to be affiliated to the Ulster Union in the near future.

Those present to form a temporary Committee until the first General Meeting, Mr. Guy acting as Hon. Secretary and Mr. Taylor as Hon. Assistant Secretary and Mr. Sharpe as Hon. Treasurer. Mr. Moorehead proposed that a "Treasure Hunt" be organised as these seemed popular in Omagh, and after discussion he and Mr. McSorley agreed to find out if one of these hunts already partly organised be merged into a larger one under the auspices of Omagh and District M.C. and the proceeds given to the Tyrone County Hospital.

A Meeting was arranged for the following Friday the 5th August but owing to the non-attendance of some of the members it was subsequently arranged to hold a meeting on Friday, 12th August at 8.00 p.m.

Mr. GUY, Hon. Secretary

Omagh and District Motor Club 1938

A General Meeting of the members of the above that was held in the Townhall, Omagh on Friday evening the 28th October, 1938. Mr. .A. G. A. Davidson, President.

Mr. T. W. Guy and Mr. Sharpe who had acted as Pro. tem Hon. Secretary and Hon. Treasurer respectively read them their reports which were accepted.

Mr. W. Donnellan gave a short address on what, he considered, were the benefits of a local motor club pointing out that the motoring outing to be organised both social and in the nature of tests and trials, which could be sub-divided to suit the ultra-enthusiast and the ordinary keen motorist. He further pointed out that while the immediate necessity for co-ordination amongst motorists did not perhaps suit, no one knew when such a need might arise and then there was no better way to meet it than by a united front.

The following members were present:
Messrs S. Moorehead, Cresswell, Fullerton, G. Johnston, Guy, Sharpe, J. W. Johnston, J. McMillin, J. S. Cunningham, S. S. Wilson, I. Leitch, Dowling, W. Donnellan, A. Davidson and G. Murnaghan.

Dr. B. Lagan was unanimously elected President. The following officers were appointed: Chairman, A.G.A. Davidson; Hon. Treas., W. Donnellan; Hon. Sec. G. Murnaghan.
The following Committees were appointed by ballot of the members present:
Ordinary Committee: Messrs Leitch, M. Mullen, Cunningham, Johnston, W. H. Fyffe, Guy, J. W. Johnston, S. S. Wilson, Sharpe and Cresswell.

Trials Committee: Messrs M. M. Turley, M. Owens, Dowling, Guy and S. Moorehead

The Chairman, Hon. Sec and Hon. Treas. are ex. officio members of both Committees.

It was decided that the Club should be affiliated to the present body in Belfast, and the Secretary was to attend to this, first ascertaining what period was covered by the subscription.

It was also decided that the Club's financial year should end on 31st December and the first financial year should be treated as ending on 31st December, 1939. The annual meeting would be held in the month of February of which members would receive a week's notice.

From the Minutes of Omagh Motor Club

It was also decided that if any of the events run by the Club members would be treated preferentially in the matter of entrance fees. For ordinary runs the charge to be 2/6 for members, 3/6 for non-members.

It was further decided if possible to have a run on 16 November, the matter to be left in the hands of the Secretary and Trials Committee.

A letter from Messrs Dowling and Leitch to the Pro tem. Secretary intimating that they had pleasure in *presenting a Cup for the next run by the Club was read*, the thanks of the Club on the generosity of these two members was tendered to them in person.

1st Cup presented to Club 1938

Minutes of A.G.M. — 3rd March, 1966

The A.G.M. was held in the Royal Arms Hotel on the 3rd March. There were approxmately 50 members present. Due to the sudden and tragic death of our Chairman Jimmy Devlin a few days previously Mervyn Armstrong kindly consented to take the chair.

The Chairman opened the meeting and made reference in some detail to our late Chairman and very good friend Jimmy Devlin. After his opening speech he called on the secretary to read the minutes of the last A.G.M. Read minutes of the 1964 A.G.M. and on those being put to the meeting were passed and signed by the Chairman and Secretary.

The Treasurer Mr. R Smith then presented the Treasurer's Report which showed the Club to be in a sound financial position. It was proposed by H. Reilly, Secretary by R. G. English that the report should be adopted.

The Secretary then presented his report on the past year's event which showed a general increase in Competition for all events. On the proposal of Peter Johnston, seconded by Bertie Bann the report was adopted.

The next business was the election of officers and resulted as follows:

PRESIDENT	Walter Hart	Pro. P Johnston	Sec. K. Graham
VICE PRESIDENT	Harry Reilly	Pro. K. Graham	Sec. R. English
CHAIRMAN	Dr. H. Mitchell	Pro. M. Armstrong	Sec. B. Bann
SECRETARY	H. P. Johnston	Pro. K. Graham	Sec. G. Currie
TREASURER	D. P. O'Connor	Pro. K. Graham	Sec. B. Bann

COMMITTEE:

R. G. English	M. D. McCann		
J. M. W. Armstrong	R. Smith		
J. Rankin	I. Allen		
W. B. Bann	F. P. Johnston	Pro. H. Reilly	
K. Graham	W. Saulters	Sec. R. J. Preston	
G. Currie	B. Burton		
J. Hunt	J. J. McAleer		

Cars owned over the years by the Crawford family of Crawford & Wilson

Top:
A pre-war Austin 10
(JI 5444)

Middle:
A post-war Vauxhall
(JI 7412)

Bottom:
A Vauxhall Wyvern
(HZ 2466)

Motoring

*Bushwhacker Rally 2002. Gary Milligan (Clerk of the Course) left
and Hugh McDaid (Scrutineer and Club Chairman).*

*The start of the rally at Molly Sweeney's on the Gortin Road in September 2002. Crews
gathering to make the final plans and adjustments before signing on with the starters.*

COMPETITOR'S NUMBER .... 84..............

ENTERED IN CLASS **3**

ULSTER AUTOMOBILE CLUB

* ★ *

Circuit of Ireland Trial

════ *24th till 27th March, 1951* ════

ROAD BOOK

ENTRANT'S NAME .... N R J. WILSON..............

ADDRESS .... CARLISLE VILLAS..............

.... Omagh..............

PARTICULARS OF CAR

MAKE .... ROVER............... TYPE .... '75'

REGISTRATION No. MZ. 4040 CHASSIS NO. O 430 3019 ENGINE NO. O 4303 052

NUMBER OF SPARE WHEELS CARRIED....... 1

The road book for the 1951 Circuit of Ireland Trial used by Norman Wilson driving a Rover '75'. In 1951, competitors were allowed passengers. In this case the passengers were Harold Wilson and Phil Richardson and the co-driver was James Bann. Their starting point was Belfast and they finished the trial.

Fuel Economy Run 1965 — Results

No.	Name	Make	Class	Forecast M.P.G.	T.	C.	Qr.	Actual M.P.G.	H'cap. M.P.G.	Placing
1	P. Johnston	Ford Corsair	3	55.876	1	2	1	49.695	55.286	3rd Class 3.
2	L. Stewart	Singer Gazelle	3	54.000	1	3	3	61.125	72.586	1st Class 3.
3	W. McFarlane	Vauxhall	3	—	1	2	3	48.512	55.183	
4	K. E. Caswell	Morris	2	53.000		19	1	49.294	47.446	
5	Mrs. Wilson	Victor 101	3	42.000	1	2	2	45.278	50.937	
6	Mrs. Vaughan	Renault 1100	2	40.000		18	1	46.307	42.255	
7	K. W. Atkinson	Ford	2	45.650		18	0	46.660	41.994	3rd Forecasters
8	B. W. J. Burton	Victor	3	35.500	1	3	2	32.513	38.203	
9	W. Knox	Ford Anglia	2	53.500		18	3	60.520	56.738	
10	P. J. Winters	Corsair	3	55.000	1	2	0	51.801	56.981	2nd Class 3.
11	P. Rutledge	Singer Vogue	3	—	1	3	2	37.966	44.609	
12	J. P. Robinson (Jun.)	Viva	2	61.500		18	3	52.694	49.401	
13	W. McLaughlin	Viva	2	46.500		17	2	46.307	40.518	1st Forecasters
14	D. Turkington	Corsair	3	42.500	1	4	3	30.563	37.821	
15	J. D. Humphries	Morris Mini	1	47.000		16	2	59.926	49.439	
16	R. G. English	Riley	3	—	1	6	3	41.582	55.616	
17	I. Coote	Austin 1100	2	54.800	1	2	1	67.170	74.727	3rd Class 2.
18	R. J. White	Hillman	3	42.000	1	3	1	40.214	46.748	
19	F. Chesney	Austin Mini	1	67.000		16	0	100.205	80.164	1st Class 1.
20	V. Lecky	Mini Minor	1	59.000		15	3	80.428	63.470	2nd Class 1.
21	D. Hamilton	M.G. Midget	2	47.000		16	3	40.214	33.679	
22	E. Flood	Citroen	4	38.000	1	8	2	Retired		
23	T. McCaughey	Ford	3	38.500	1	2	2	36.822	41.425	
24	W. M. Saulters	Morris 1100	2	53.000		19	2	56.597	55.182	
25	R. F. B. Griffin	Triumph Herald	5	48.400	1	1	3	52.694	57.305	1st Class 5.
26	J. Moore	Morris 1100	2	39.000		19	1	41.866	40.296	
27	T. Hobson	Mini	1	56.400		15	2	55.068	42.677	
28	T. R. Boyd	Ford Corsair	3	—	1	1	1	40.750	43.297	
29	G. H. Scott	Fait	1	—		14	2	55.568	40.286	
30	G. B. Kay	Volkswagen	2	—		19	0	46.307	43.991	
31	J. Cunningham	Renault 4L	1	63.000		15	2	65.027	50.395	
32	Thelma Loane	Austin Mini	1	58.700		15	0	62.372	46.779	
33	J. Hamilton	Imp	2	45.600		16	3	59.345	49.701	
34	P. O'Goan	Austin 7	1	—		14	3	55.068	40.613	
35	R. Pollock	Viva	2	—		18	1	46.307	42.255	
36	E. Bennett	Imp	2	48.800		18	1	43.351	39.558	
37	I. Caldwell	Mini	1	55.500		15	2	67.917	52.635	3rd Class 1.
38	G. McLaren	Mini	1	—		15	3	80.428	63.470	
39	H. Armstrong	Mini	1	50.000		15	1	55.568	42.370	
40	J. A. Eakin	Austin	4	—	1	5	2	67.917	86.593	1st Class 4, 1st H'cap.
41	O. Hadden	Ford	3	—	1	2	2	41.301	46.463	
42	P. McAleer	Victor	3	57.000	1	3	2	49.294	57.920	
43	M. Johnston	Austin Cooper	5	48.000		18	1	44.293	40.418	
44	M. Vance	Volkswagen	2	—		19	3	38.203	37.726	
45	Mrs. Rankin	Austin Cooper	2	45.320		15	2	70.259	53.731	1st Class 2. 1st Ladies
46	H. Johnston	Austin	2	71.000		17	1	68.680	59.236	2nd Class 2
47	D. McBride	Imp	2	63.500		16	2	63.015	51.987	2nd Forecasters
48	Mrs. E. Bell	Victor	3	42.300	1	3	2	33.771	39.680	
49	N. Bell	Vauxhall 101	3	31.900	1	2	2	29.387	33.060	
50	C. Beattie	Cortina	2	49.700		19	2	47.384	46.199	
51	R. McCartney	Renault	2	62.000	1	0	2	64.342	65.950	
52	R. Armstrong	Volkswagen	2	50.600		18	1	43.046	39.279	
53	S. Raphael	Imp	2	—		16	2	52.244	43.100	
54	R. D. J. Sloan	A.60	4	40.500	1	5	2	48.900	62.347	
55	S. Kearney	Ford 998	2	60.000		19	3	53.152	52.488	
56	B. Little	Austin Mini	1	66.000		16	3	49.695	41.620	
57	E. O'Hagan	Anglia	2	—		18	2	35.956	33.259	
58	J. Thompson	Morris Cooper	2	38.000		15	1	46.307	35.309	
59	D. McCann	Saab	1	22.500		18	3	32.003	30.003	

PETROL SUPPLIED FREE BY MEX

Austin Owners

Raymond Anderson and son Lee in full funeral gear in front of their restored 1925 Austin 20/4 Hearse at Kilbroney in 2004. The only one of this model in N. Ireland. Coach Builder: Thomas Startin Jnr. Ltd.   Ref. Vol. 13, page 240

Some more Austins in the Anderson Collection.
(l to r): 1933 Austin L 12/4 Harley Saloon (Dublin registered); 1928 Austin H 12/4 Clifton Tourer (early years, McKenna Bros., Aughnacloy); 1927 Austin 20/4 Hackney Carriage (8 seater limosine). Coachwork by J. C. Clarke Ltd., London (once a London taxi).

Austins at Omagh Carnival on 23rd June, 2006. Godfrey Crawford's 1926 Austin 20/4 Ascot Saloon with divider. Originally from Monaghan. Restored over a 11 year period.

Followed by Marshall Fenton's Austin (H/12) Heavy Twelve. Body by Salmons & Sons, Tickford (all-weather saloon). Only three known of this model. To operate the hood you put the starting handle in back rear side corner and wind down.

CHAPTER 5

The History of Tyrone Farming Society
by William McGrew in 1989

Thumbnail Sketches of
Omagh (now Tyrone) Farming Society's Annual Show

With the announcement that the Tyrone Farming Society was to celebrate its one hundred and fiftieth show in 1989, it was decided to write up a short history of this popular event in the Spring of that year. Programmes, photos, and interviews with show officials were felt to be necessary to achieve this.

One well known retired businessman, Mr. William Armstrong of Campsie Road, was visited. Mr. Armstrong was for many years one of the judges of the "Show" but unfortunately — disaster — his house and shop which were badly wrecked in a bomb attack some years ago were devastated so badly that his programmes, notes, and photos were utterly destroyed. A Miss Johnston of Seskinore, who had been secretary's clerk for some years, was paid a visit but unfortunately did not possess any programmes either.

A well known local gentleman, Harry Sproule, now deceased, did excellent work in setting up the "props" for the Show each year. A relative was called on to see if she had anything which would be of help, only to be told that after Harry died she had cleared out all his trophies and dumped them. This was a great disappointment and when told that she would have been paid for any of this, she said "If I had known that they would have been of use to you, you could have had them for nothing". Other persons with links to the Show were approached for programmes, etc, but with the same expressions of regret, they had nothing.

Omagh, Strabane, Clogher Farming Society "To the Best Cow" on 16th August, 1849.

History of Tyrone Farming Society

While this was going on several visits were paid to the offices of the Tyrone Constitution, taking notes on the Show from old issues of the paper, at random. It was felt that perhaps some write-up to celebrate the 50th and 100th anniversaries in 1889 and 1939 respectively, may have been found for those years. 1889 drew a blank — no show! — but when 1939 was checked, a surprise was in store — there was a Show that year all right, but it was the 107th Show.

To be certain that this was correct, the 1932 paper was looked up, and there it was: the Tyrone Farming Society celebrated its centenary of the Show. Checking through the "Con" it was found that the Show was not held every year. There were times when it failed to appear, so with that and the knowledge that 1989 was in reality the 157th anniversary of the formation of this event, it was decided to forget it.

The notes from the Con were scattered in two notebooks and various pieces of paper and recently it was decided to destroy them. However, it was decided to put them together in chronological order, as it was felt that they might be of interest to someone — perhaps a future local historian doing a book on the Omagh Show in the year 2032 to celebrate its bi-centenary might use some of it. Although the anniversary date was seven years out, the officers and committee of the Tyrone Farming Society may find it of some comfort to realise that the Show is actually older than they estimated and will only have to wait 43 years to celebrate its 200th anniversary, for in the year 2032 when people are booking their holidays on one of the moons of Saturn at Belfast Universal Spaceport, others will be looking forward to visiting the "Omagh Show", still going strong.

The earliest records are:
June 1832, when at a meeting of the committee of the Omagh Farming Society (as it was known) there was a poor attendance and no one would came forward to take the offices of

At the Tyrone Farming Society Show on 5th July, 1939.
(l to r): Col. Galbraith, Sir Basil Brooke, David Clements and William Walsh.

Tyrone Farming Society
OFFICERS 1949

President:
The Marquis of Hamilton

Vice-Presidents
W. E. Orr   Lt-Col. R. R. A. Darling
Capt. W. Maddin Scott   John Cathcart
Patrick Cunningham, M.P.
Col. J. M. Blakiston-Houston
T. H. O'Doherty

Life Member
Miss M. A. Lawson

Executive Committee
Chairman: **Capt. W. Maddin Scott**
Vice-Chairman: **Patrick Cunningham, Esq.**, M.P.

W. A. Armstrong	**William Watson**
R. Henderson	**N. R. J. Wilson**, J.P.
John Lyons	**J. R. McMillin**
James Crammond	**John Clements**
William Given	**N. A. Donaghy**
T. Dunn., M.R.C.V.S.	**Jack Devlin**
R. H. Johnston, J.P.	**D. Barbour**
H. A. J. Kyle	**S. Busby**
W. M. Shilliday J. L. McKelvey J. D. Watson, J.P.	

Managing Committee
Chairman: **Capt. W. Maddin Scott**
Vice-Chairman: **Patrick Cunningham**, J.P.

Cmdr. J. C. Hayes	**Major Teasdale**
James G. Allen	**Thomas Farrell**
D. McKenzie	**T. Crammond**
A. T. Blair	**W. Johnston**
William Walsh	**Alex McKimmon**
R. J. Watson	**W. H. Kyle**
Cecil White	**J. Rainey**
W. J. Wilson	**J. R. A. Pollock**
Capt. W. R. Fyffe, O.B.E.	**Alex Logan**
Frank McCanny	**J. Campbell**
R. Wauchob, M.R.C.V.S.	**A. Alcorn**
J. S. Rountree	**Robert Mitchell**
M. F. McSorley	**W. F. Porter**
Thomas Marshall	**R. W. J. Waterson**
Harold M. McCauley	**William Thomson**
William Lyons	**Joseph McConnell**
Michael Cunningham	**A. Cummins**
Charles Beattie, J.P.	**Capt. Chambers**, M.C.
L. Fowler W. Hamilton T. B. Kee T. S. Clarke	
Samuel Robinson	**John McGrath**
F. Teague Millar Hamilton	**C. V. McAleer**

Hon. Veterinary Surgeons
T. E. Johnston, M.R.C.V.S., **Fintona**
J. Adams, M.R.C.V.S., **Omagh**
F. Mullan, M.R.C.V.S., **Omagh**
E. Wauchob, M.R.C.V.S., **Newtownstewart**

Hon. Treasurers
Provincial bank, Omagh

Hon. Auditors
H. B. Brandon, Jamison & Co., Omagh

Hon. Secretaries
Fred J. Johnston, 45 High Street, Omagh
Roy B. Holmes, John Street, Omagh

Secretary
William J. Beatty, 59 High Street, Omagh

Omagh Annual Show

Dance

In the
STAR BALLROOM
Wednesday, 6th July, '49
Dancing 9 till 2

ADMISSION   -   -   LADIES, 4/- GENTLEMEN, 5/-

ADVERTISEMENTS.

DAVID BROWN
The Most Economic Tractor Yet

are you buying a Diesel ?

DAVID BROWN 25D

NOW only £558

* David Brown Direct Injection Engine
* Quick-fire starting
* 6-speed gearbox 1·5-15 m.p.h.
* Independent foot brakes

ORDER WITH THE MAIN DEALERS NOW

JAMES EAKIN & SONS
DUBLIN ROAD, OMAGH
Phone: Omagh 21

History of Tyrone Farming Society

Honorary Secretary and Treasurer, who had resigned their places. It was then decided to call a special meeting of the subscribers, on 24th of the same month in the White Hart Hotel (now the site of the Post Office) to appoint two officers to act for the ensuing year and failing that to consider dissolving the Society, but it was earnestly hoped to get the matter settled as it was felt that the Society was performing a useful function.

The matter was happily settled at this last meeting with the appointment of Mr. John G. R. Porter as Treasurer and Messrs. W. H. Kyle and J. J. Gilmour as the joint Secretaries, resulting in the show being held on the 25th July in the flax market (now the site of the car park area for the Omagh salesyard to the rear of the Gospel Hall). The Committee had dinner in the Royal Arms Hotel afterwards. (Commencing time for above Show — 11.00 a.m.)
Omagh Cattle Show — 28th August 1856 — Hon. Sec., Corry Coulson, Camowen.
Show for 1852 held on 21st August — Mr. M. Armstrong replaced John Carson as Hon. Secretary. (George Hall Stack — Vice-President.)

23rd July, 1884 — Horse jumping show, again in the flax market area.
Tyrone Farming Society — 1st December, 1912 — Horse and Cattle show in new grounds.
1915 Secretary — James Johnston.

After the show in 1939, because of war-time measures, the Omagh Showgrounds in Sedan Avenue, where the show was now being held, was taken over by the military for a period of nearly eight years. No show, but a gymkhana, sports and dog show were held in the Showgrounds under the patronage of Capt. Madden Scott in the years 1944 and '45.

31st July 1946 — Permission was given to hold a gymkhana and horse show in the Showgrounds in aid of the Royal Inniskilling Fusiliers, the Royal Ulster Rifles and the Royal Irish Fusiliers. Musical entertainment was provided by the pipes and drums of 25th ITC, under Pipe-Major McIntyre.

1946 – Mr. W. J. Beattie appointed secretary (to 1967).

9th July, 1947 — First Show after wartime, 108th. It was wildly successful and was described as being in some ways superior to exhibits at Balmoral and Ballsbridge. Hundreds came by car in what was a record attendance. Among those present were the Marquis and Marchioness of Hamilton, Commandant Finlay of the Eire army, etc. Mr. Jack Mather of

Judging cattle in the 1950s.

History of Tyrone Farming Society

Portadown brought three distinguished Turkish officers, one of whom, Captain C. N. Akim, acted as interpretator (sic). These latter were there with a view of purchasing good jumping horses.

President **Marquis of Hamilton**
Vice-President **Mr. P. Cunningham,** M.P.
Chairman **Lt-Col. Galbraith,** O.B.E.

6th July, 1949 — Additional attraction was a parade of hounds of Seskinore Hunt Club which had been re-formed by Mr. B. R. W. Bell and Major W. R. Cairns, Kings Dragoon Guards. Music by KDG band under Mr. R. H. Jarvis, A.R.C.M.

5th July, 1950 — Gymkhana in afternoon and sports. St. Eugene's Brass and Reed Band in attendance under Mr. Bryan Turbitt. Red Cross in action, three casualties. Dance in Star Ballroom that night, courtesy of the Show. The Carlton Dance Band played the music. Admission 5 shillings (equals 25p nowadays). On a sad note, Lt-Col. Galbraith dies on 1st October that year.

6th July, 1955 — Canadian Government had a display stand at the Show. Dog show and poultry competition sections. Catering by Carlisle Restaurant. Music by St. Eugene's Brass and Reed Band. Duke and Duchess of Abercorn present. W. J. Beattie, secretary and Mr. F. J. J. Johnston and Mr. R. B. Holmes, Joint Honorary Secretaries.

1st July, 1959 — Lord Wakehurst, Governor of Northern Ireland, was guest of honour at this year's Show. Heavy rain fell all day but failed to put a damper on enthusiasm of either contestants or spectators.

Parade of prize-winning cattle in the 1950s.

History of Tyrone Farming Society

5th and 6th July, 1960 — Show time which to this year had been one day event (Wednesday) now extended to one and a half days — afternoon Tuesday and all day Wednesday.

3rd and 4th July, 1962 — Captain John Brooke was one of the distinguished visitors. Ninety-two year old Mr. James Mulligan, who had been a regular visitor to the Show, was unable to attend but sent sons Robin and William along to enter prize sheep in contest, collected 8 firsts, 5 seconds and 3 third prizes. Mr. William Greer — official collector.

6th and 7th July, 1965 — Mr R. B. Holmes, former secretary, in an interview with the press remembered the days when Strabane had a two day show and trade exhibits, but because of lack of interest attendance fell off to such an extent that only two spectators showed up at the last Show there and it had to be discontinued. He also imparted the information that the first catering to the Omagh Show was provided by Messrs. W. & C. Scott who treated customers and interested parties to hot bowls of porridge.

1969 — Mr. R. Holmes, former Secretary of Show, died in January.

1971 — Show venue further extended to two day event — Tuesday and Wednesday.

1974 — Dates for venue switched to Friday and Saturday.

1984 — Show further extended to Thursday, Friday and Saturday, three days.

1985 — Secretary was Mr. R. A. (Bertie) Pollock. He had held this post since 1968.

1988 — President: Duke of Abercorn. Chairman: Mr. W. A. Mooney. Secretary: Mr. Bertie Pollock. Former secretary Mr. W. J. Beattie died on 27th November. Mr. Beattie was also well known in rugby circles internationally, being the founder member of Omagh Academicals Rugby Club, in which he maintained a keen interest up to his demise. Popularly known as the "The Beat".

U. EQUINOX

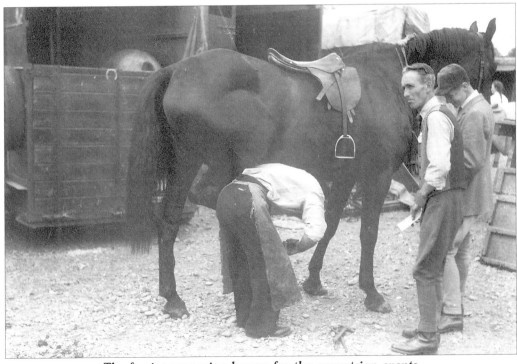

The farrier preparing horses for the equestrian events.

Tribute to Billy Beatty
by Harry McCartney

The address given to the Omagh Academicals Rugby Club by Harry McCartney on Sunday 4th December, 1988 at the Mellon Park Playing Fields on the occasion of the scattering of the ashes of the late Secretary William J. Beatty by the Rev. K. Kingston in the presence of his sisters, club members and friends.

Billy Beatty

Ladies and gentlemen it is with sadness that we are gathered here this afternoon to pay final tribute to an old and esteemed friend Billy Beatty.

"Friend after friend departs
Who has not lost a friend?
There is no union here of hearts
That friends not here an end"

I feel sure that most of us have by now read the tribute to Billy in the local press. His life and career had been well chronicled in print and so it is no disrespect or lack of appreciation that I omit or touch lightly on a number of things.

(i)   We know of Billy's highly successful career in business founded upon hard work, honesty and integrity. We remember him for his efficiency and organising ability as secretary of Omagh Show.

(ii) The Newspaper report refers to him as a *Rugby Legend* and this is no exaggeration for he was known throughout Ulster and indeed further afield for his warm and genial personality and his work for rugby football, as a player, club secretary and selector for Town or Ulster.

(iii) As past Captain of Omagh Golf Club he was held in high esteem and many of us will remember him as an active member of Omagh Water Ski Club.

(iv) Outside sport and business, Billy's interests were many and varied. The largest congregation attending the funeral services in St. Columba's Parish Church and Roselawn Crematorium bore witness to his popularity.

Pascal the 17th century French philosopher and poet somewhat cynically wrote
"Life consists but of 3 things . . . Birth, Life and Death.

We feel not Birth, we suffer Death and we forget to Live. Regrettably in the final weeks of life Billy was to suffer much pain which he endured with that certain 'Grittyness" and strength of spirit which was so typical of the man.

The gathering of club members for the scattering and address by Harry McCartney.

Tribute to Billy Beatty

Harry McCartney

And here in passing may I pay tribute to the love, care and devotion of his sisters Clara and Doreen throughout his lengthy illness.

But let us not dwell upon his death but rather on his life for Billy certainly did not forget how to live. Few people enjoyed life more, yet it was not a selfish, hedonistic life for there was always behind the open friendliness and rumbustious good humour a charitable caring and generous man, indeed in many ways a modest man.

We remember the familiar figure "running the touchline" of the 1st XV rugby pitch and wobetide the spectator who would trespass but one step onto the field of play.

We remember the friendship and camaraderie in the clubhouse after the game for where Billy was concerned there were no strangers simply friends who he had yet to meet. As we yarn with friends over a drink our eyes wander around the room to the fields beyond. We pause and remember that these fine premises, these pitches are ours thanks to the foresight, work and dedication of our late club secretary Billy Beatty — the Beat. It was he who many years ago took the initiative of writing to the club's benefactor in America, Thomas Mellon: it was Billy who was first on the scene to help the building contractor unload the bricks, to mix the mortar, to lay the foundations. This pavilion was his vision and as long as brick and steel stand it will remain a fitting memorial.

For Billy rugby was always "King of Sports". By its nature however it is a very physical sport and occasionally fatal and serious injuries do occur. Tragedy has struck twice in the history of our club. A young man died another was crippled – both as a result of injuries on the field of play. On those occasions we were witness to the caring and sympathetic side of Billy's nature. In illness and death Billy was always there to offer sympathy and support, no bedside was too far away to visit, no effort was spared to lend a helping hand.

As we know and remember him Billy was a charitable and generous man. His generousity will be specially remembered in rugby circles. Few visitors travelling a distance to the rugby club left without benefiting from his hospitality. Many a meal was ordered and personally paid for by Billy: many a banknote was thrust into the hand of a young player to buy a round of refreshments when on tour; many a friend's debt was quietly settled without any thought of its repayment.

Billy, as I mentioned was in many ways a modest self-effacing person — modest in life-style modest about success and achievement. Hard work for and around the rugby club sought no praise and very little recognition. Not only was he club secretary but sometimes self-appointed groundsman. Compliments on the state of the grounds or in improvements in the pavilion would often be met with a shrug of the shoulders or a nod of the head as if to say "Things have to be done around here". Billy was justly proud of the rugby club but he was never egotistical for he believed that the club was as much yours and mine as his and the only demands he would make upon us was our support for the club and our respect for the premises.

Far off fields hold and attraction for more of us. Billy was no exception. He travelled widely yet "Tyrone among the bushes" always beckoned him home. He was always happiest in Omagh, his birth place, the town he loved. It is fitting therefore in accordance with his wishes his ashes should be scattered on the playing field of his beloved rugby club. After the ceremony it was also his wish that we his friends should meet informally to chat and reminisce about times past, times present and times to be.

Through Billy may I therefore invite you later to drink together a cup for the sake of Auld Lang Syne.

"Friends depart and memory takes them to her cavern pure and deep"

Let us cherish these memories.

Thank you!

The scattering of the ashes by the Rev. Kingston.

For years the showgrounds was the venue for a popular market on Mondays.

The Showgrounds was the venue for regular monthly machinery sales.
Edmund Wiltshire (deceased) with auctioneer Pat O'Kane in 1993.

History of Tyrone Farming Society

The showgrounds was sold in 2002 and a retail park developed.

A new showgrounds with permanent offices and two equestrian arenas was built on the Drumquin Road. The photograph shows the 2006 Show Officials — Secretary Mr. Cartwright, horseman Richard Smith, representative of David Prentice (main sponsors), David Stewart (Veterinary Surgeon) Chairman and John Chambers, designer of horse jumping course and Omagh's only representative at the last Olympic Games in Germany and the European Games in Aachen, Germany 2006.

W. J. JOHNSTON'S
THE CALIFORNIA HOUSE

In the early years of the last century, Fred and Jim Johnston ran one of the best known draper shops in the County, but their first love was farming and the Tyrone Farming Society honoured them both with illuminated addresses over the years. Firstly, Jim for his post as Secretary and secondly, Fred on the occasion of his marriage.

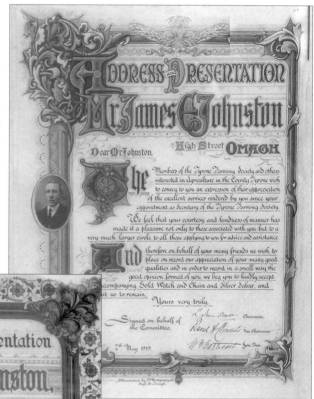

*Ronnie Orr and Bertie Pollock (long term Secretary of the T.F.S.)
discussing the affairs of the 2006 Show.*

Celebrating 100 Years of the Home Industries section at the 2006 Show.

CHAPTER 6

World War II

When World War II broke out in 1939 Lisanelly Barracks did not exist. The land was requisitioned from the Murnaghan family and quickly constructed with the first recruits arriving during 1940.

They were put through a 6 weeks to 3 months course of training depending on their postings and having arrived in civilian clothes they left in their army uniforms.

The Americans arrived in Seskinore in October 1943 and remained in and around Omagh until the D-Day Landings on 6th June, 1944.

It was not until after the war and the Camp re-opened after a period of closure that British regiments came to do periods of service here usually on an average of about 2¹/₂ years at a time. This ended with the K.O.S.Bs leaving in September 2006.

As quick as they came, all signs of the American presence disappeared soon after the war was over. The only building I can relate to the Americans is close to the Knock-na-Moe stables and that building was used as a laundry.

Photograph courtesy of Gerry Devlin

The American laundry in the grounds of Knock-na-Moe Castle.
The only building still standing in Omagh that the Americans used during World War II.

World War II

Inniskillings Pipe Band at the Courthouse for the opening of the Spring Assizes.

Guard of Honour waiting to be inspected by the visiting judge.

A group of NAAFI catering staff at St. Lucia Barracks in the 1940s.

A large group of recruits enjoying themselves at St. Lucia Barracks during the war years.

A common scene in Omagh during the war years was a military brass band with a battalion marching behind it through the main streets of the town to the various Camps.

A group of soldiers having just finished their training and won the Platoon Cup.

Keeping fit with many sports was part of a soldier's training and boxing was very popular both to take part in and to watch. The gymnasium at St. Lucia was a frequent venue.

A bicycle race about to start in the Military Holm.
It is probably a slow race as most of the competitors are in uniform.

World War II

The majority of the Americans in the Omagh area came in October 1943 and left quickly in May 1944 for the south of England to prepare for the D-Day Landings on 6th June, 1944. They loved being photographed and Kenneth Crane was only too happy to oblige.

Many Omagh families invited the troops into their homes even the German P.O.Ws. This group on the river bank in Campsie are guests of the Conway and McGale families. Back Row (l to r): Mickey Conway, Frank McGale, Paddy McAlinney, G.I., G.I., Jim Conway. Front Row (l to r): G.I., G.I., Billy Ball, G.I., Children: Clare Armstrong and Harry McGale.

A parade leaving Lisanelly in the 1940s. This is the same entrance that is used today.

Some of the cavalry regiments brought their horses (and even their dogs) to Omagh.
Shown here are the Lancers.

An armed patrol at the main entrance in the 1940s. Note the houses on the main Gortin Road on the left and the Omagh Workhouse top left.

Presentation of a group shield after a cross-country race in the Camp grounds.

*The ATS had their barracks opposite Lisanelly where the Silverbirch Hotel is today —
some of the buildings still remain.
Male and female army personnel parading and receiving their shamrocks on
St. Patrick's Day in the 1940s.*

Civilian Volunteers

Omagh's Auxiliary Fire Service photographed in the Crescent Dairy area of Campsie Avenue 1940.
Back Row (l to r):   Jack McMillin, Jimmy Reilly, John Torrens, Alfie Johnston.
Front Row (l to r):   Jack Devlin, Marcus Pigott, Jack Torrens, Walter McGaughey.

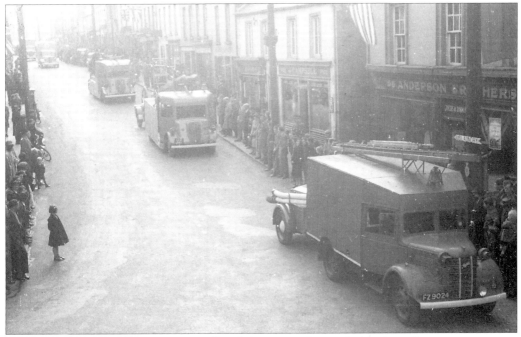

After the war came the victory parades and street parties.
This parade on V.E. Day 1945 down Market Street is of the Fire Tenders and
Ambulances all manned by local men on a voluntary basis over the war years.

Civilian Volunteers

No. 8 Platoon 'B' Company (2nd Tyrone Battalion) Ulster Home Guard photographed in the grounds of Omagh Academy.

Front Row (l to r): Cpl. J. Dolan, Sgt. M. J. McCutcheon, P/Sgt. S. J. Johnston, 2/Lieut. J. O. H. Long, R.M. Sgt. R. H. Pyne, Sgt. T. Gilliland, Vol. J. Duncan.

Middle Row (l to r): Volunteers T. Stewart, J. Bible, M. Duff, G. Thompson, S. McNickle, J. Jeffrey.

Back Row (l to r): Volunteers G. Kerr, C. Camley, M. Coyle, W. Potts, A. Thompson, G. Mullan, C. Leitch, H. Kerr.

Civilian Volunteers

A.R.P (Air Raid Precautions) and First Aid (1940) in Academy grounds with ambulance and cars.

Back Row (l to r): Soldier (South Wales Borderers), F. J. Johnston, Harry Brown, Charles Donaghy, Jack Graham, J. Dick, William Ballantine, ——, Jim Moffitt, Ollie Clements, — Cupples, ——, H. Todd, J. Morrison, ——, Robert Mitchell, Soldier (South Wales Borderers).

Front Row (l to r): — Farren, J. Reid, H. McCrumlish, ——, Gordon Preston, Dr. F. C. J. Mitchell, Dr. Bernard Logan, ——, Archie Burton, J. McCusker, Herbie Kyle, P. Meeghan, ——.

85

Weddings — before, during and after World War II

Crevenagh Farm c.1903 — the marriage of Elise Adams to Doctor James Hunt. Elise later became a dermatologist and practised in Leeds. Two of her sisters, Frances and Minnie, started the well known school in the High Street which amalgamated with the Academy in 1920.

The marriage of Beatrice Mitchell and Omagh solicitor Stanley Rountree at First Omagh Presbyterian Church. The bridesmaid was Sylvia McFarland and the best man Capt. C. N. M. Rountree. The pages were Maida McVicker (Ballymena) and the compiler himself.

Weddings — before, during and after World War II

The wedding of John A. Cathcart and Florence Anderson, Innishfree, Derry Road, Omagh in St. Columba's, Church of Ireland on Tuesday, 2nd June, 1942.

Married at Ballynahatty Presbyterian Church on 15th June, 1949 by Rev. Ernest Cochrane were Clarke Campbell, Kevlin House and Rosanna Monteith of Mullaghmore, Ballynahatty. This was one of the last weddings in the church which is now demolished.

The bridal car in true fashion taking the newly weds off down Church Street.

Weddings — before, during and after World War II

*The wedding of Jack Campbell, Kevlin House and Rubena McKimmon,
Drumshanley in St. Columba's, Church of Ireland on 29th September 1943.*

Bertie Parke and Olive Stewart marry on 2nd September, 1948.

Weddings — before, during and after World War II

Tommy Gilliland marries Miss Leitch of Coolnagard at St. Columba's, Church of Ireland on 24th April 1940.

Constable Robert Spence marries Miss Margaret Gilmour of Drumshiel, Dromore at Trinity Pres. Church.

(l to r): Best Man: Milton Stewart, Cecil Stewart and Lily McMichael and Bridesmaid: Eva Dunne (née McMichael).

Weddings — before, during and after World War II

Sam Hooke marries Frances E. Irwin of Sedan Avenue, Omagh.

Tom Colvin marrying Susan McKee (of the Cake Shop).

Harold McCauley and Gertie Duff marry in Enniskillen on 1st June, 1948.

Annabell Lucinda Beattie and Richard Wilton, 82 Market Street wed on the 19th May, 1944.

CHAPTER 7

Omagh's Town Hall

When the auditorium of the Town Hall opened in 1915, Omagh gained a very eye-catching building for the next 82 years. It had roof lighting from two large skylights and a central dome — there were no windows in the outer walls which allowed for control of outside light during daytime performances.

A lot of credit for this building must go to the Urban Council of the day. They had leased the old Ulster Bank building in 1909 and converted the front portion for their own use which was to develop over the years as the town grew and required more facilities.

The auditorium was built at the rear of the High Street premises and opened on the 29th September, 1915.

The architect was John M. Robinson, Derry and the builder was Isaac Copeland, Belfast. The Clerk of Works was John Thompson.

A Minor Hall was designed not far from the main entrance and it was to play a big part in the future of the Town Hall when the larger auditorium wasn't required.

The auditorium with its distinct skylights and dome.

Omagh's Town Hall

- The centrally located dome was made by Heywood & Co. of Huddersfield.
- The attractive balcony rail was made in Glasgow by Messrs Walter MacFarlane & Co.
- The plumbing and sanitary work was by Crawford & Wilson of Omagh.
- The plumbing and lighting was carried out by the council plumber Bob Hynes.
- The manager of the Omagh Gasworks, Mr. P. J. O'Callaghan supervised the installation of the heating and ventilation which was carried out by the Belfast firm of Musgrave & Co.

The Town Hall was to be a multi-purpose building over the years of its existence. It housed the Library in its early days, the Rates Office and the Minor Hall was one of the first departments of Technical Institution.

Upstairs on the way to the main hall was the Council Chambers where the Omagh Urban Council met until the Council moved to the Grange on the Gortin Road.

During World War II both British and American servicemen were billited in different parts of the building.

Of course the main reason for the building of the hall was to have a venue where the people of Omagh could come and be entertained and this is what they most certainly got.

A view of the auditorium from the gallery.

Omagh's Town Hall

Travelling Companies from Shakespeare to Bam-Boo-Zalem drew the crowds. But it will be the May Feis and the Omagh Players that will be remembered for the many full houses they created by the competition at the Feis from over a wide area and the quality of plays, pantomimes and revues that were presented over the years.

Boxing and wrestling were also guaranteed to produce a full house, especially when local men were fighting. Cyril 'Bozo' Woods *(see photo)* from Campsie Crescent started his wrestling career in Omagh Town Hall and spread his wings

Cyril 'Bozo' Woods and his wife on a visit to Omagh in 1997.

to other venues in Ireland until he changed his name and went to North America where in due course he set up a business in Toronto and made his fortune. He still calls in to see us when he is home visiting his relatives in Omagh and Castlederg.

PTQ sellers from Queens University, Belfast at the entrance to the Town Hall in 1960.

The Omagh Library in the front left room of the Town Hall with Mrs. Eileen Coote (centre). The Library moved to the pavilion in Sedan Avenue following a bomb in the Town Hall in 1974.

POSTERS FROM THE SHOWS

"Robin Hood" • *January 1980.*

"Jesus Christ Superstar" • *Sept. 1980.*

"Stage Coach" • *February 1981.*

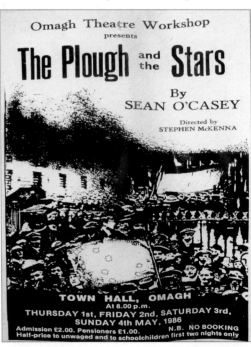

"The Plough and the Stars" • *May. 1986.*

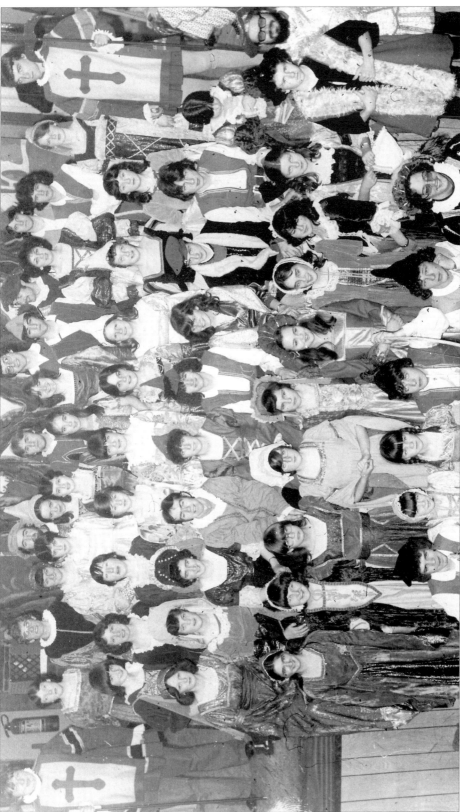

The Chorus of "Robin Hood" Pantomime in 1980.

Back Row (l to r): John McCormack, Anne Marie Bradley, Liam Moore, Lorna McLennan, Liam Foley, Rosaleen Kiruan, Marie McMulkin, Ann McCusker, Terry Sweeney, Ciara Rodgers, Rosemary Carson, Ronan Mallon, Martin Sweeney, Peter Turbitt, Concepta O'Donnell, Seamus Bonner, Eamon Gilleese, Noreen Cummins, David Douglas.

Fourth Row (l to r): Noelle McDavitt, Maria Turbitt, Yvonne Collins, Teresa Breen, Mairead Brogan, Jacqueline O'Donnell, Audrey Fisher, Lorraine Humphries, Donna McHugh.

Third Row (l to r): Mary Livingstone, Margaret O'Donnell, Pauline Rodgers, Joe Cuthbertson, Christina McGuigan, Derek Ballard, Catriona Blayney, Niall Colgan, Brendan McNabb, Josephine Hill.

Second Row (l to r): Michelle Turbitt, Nuala Mills, Siobhan Moore, Maureen Hunter, Nuala McElhinney, Ann Bresnahan, Joan Mathers, Lorraine Jackson, Noreen Gormley, Laurence O'Neill, P. A. McLaughlin.

Front Row (l to r): Kevin O'Neill, Catherine Fisher, Teresa Hill, Peter Brogan, Sean Fullerton, Mark Gavin.

95

The Cast of "The Crucible" in 1986.

Back Row (l to r):   Paul Gallagher, Brian McCann, Justin O'Doherty, Pat McAleer, John Breslin, Jimmy Fisher (dec.), Tony McGartland, Eddie McCaffrey, Owen Doody.

Middle Row (l to r):   Michael Mullan, Ronnie Moran, Audrey Fisher, Mary Martin, Phemie Glass, Baevin Bann, Briege McLaughlin, Audrey Barbour, Sophia Maguire, Orlagh Bann, Tom Riddle, Liam Brogan.

Front Row (l to r):   Gerry Norton, Pearl Fisher, Kathleen Hinds (Producer and Director).

OMAGH TOWN HALL

In 1915 you were dressed up like a queen,
When the Skins army band played you in;
The year before, began that terrible war,
You survived to see it all happen again.

Since then you became a household name,
A grand place for the Feis or a bazaar;
Where prizes were won and people had fun,
Away back in those days now afar.

Wee cubs from school stood straight as a rule,
On this stage they gave all heart and soul;
Master wasn't pleased as they coughed 'n' sneezed,
When they recited some old rigmarole.

Sure, this was the place to bring smiles to the face,
It was like home, just one big family affair;
When Mossey and Co. would stop the whole show,
With a jibe at someone sitting out there.

Remember the queues at the Easter Revues,
Remember the great concerts and plays;
When a good hypnotist made up the vast list,
And he kept the full houses in a daze.

Fighters, writers and famous one-nighters.
And great actors excelled here one time;
And were happy enough with good local stuff,
When they starred in our own pantomime.

Now inside these walls, cheers and catcalls,
Will soon fade and will then die away;
The good times we had will make us feel sad,
When we think of those times yesterday.

You are a grand oul doll, Omey Town Hall,
You've been around for over eighty-two years;
But now we will see your grand valedictory,
With some laughter, songs and some tears.

Adicu! Adieu! We will all remember you,
Long years after this curtain call;
They will never replace this hallowed space,
Fond farewell to our Omey Town Hall!

Jackie McGale

Omagh Players

A Brief History — 1934-1994

written by Kathleen Hinds on the occasion of their

Diamond Jubilee in 1994

The Omagh Players this year celebrate the 60th Anniversary of their foundation and it would be fair to say that since the autumn of 1934 when the late F. J. Nugent persuaded a few of his companions to found a drama group the Company has gone from strength to strength.

Throughout its early years, Francis Joseph, as he was affectionately known, was the driving force behind a series of productions which won for the fledgling group a growing reputation and after almost obligatory flirtation with Ulster comedy their producer turned their attention to tragedy with the emergence of the Players' first playwright Louis D. Lynch and with *"Heritage"*, a drama of recent Irish history, FJ showed his ability to cope with the demands of an even more taxing medium. *"Greater Love"* from the same pen served to consolidate the reputation of both producer and players and further triumphs were to follow as the group tackled with success *"The Coming of the Magi"* and *"A Saint in a Hurry"* a religious play based on the life of St. Francis Xavier. Indeed, this latter production was to bring the group their first success on the demanding festival circuit with the Players winning the prestigious Longford Cup, the premier award in the open class in Dundalk.

"Ring Round The Moon" — 1991
(l to r): Vincent McBride, Dermot McCormack, Kathleen Hinds, Pearl Fisher, Cahill McKenna.

Omagh Players — A Brief History

With their standing now well established not only locally where packed houses were assured at all performances, but indeed on a wider stage, the Players suffered the sort of setback that tested their resolve as due to promotion Francis Joseph, the man who had been regarded as an oracle with the group, was forced to leave the town.

Displaying the resolve that was to be indicative of their progress throughout the years the players rallied and, largely through the efforts of Rev. P. McHugh, the name of Omagh Players was kept alive mainly through revivals of past productions.

The coming of the war in 1939 proved to be a watershed in the history of the group. Despite the difficulties of this period a man arrived who was to prove a central figure in the Players' progress over the years that followed.

Paddy Bogues came to Omagh as an official with the newly established Assistance Board. From the outset of his involvement with the Players, Paddy was to prove a veritable mine of inspiration and his first production with the group *"Laburnum Grove"* revealed him as a producer of extraordinary ability. Following in the footsteps of an esteemed a character as Francis Joseph Nugent did not make life easy for Paddy but his powers of leadership and enthusiasm coupled with the continued excellence of the productions that were being turned out under his guidance won him a special place in the history of the Players.

"Andorra" — 1994
(l to r): Dermot McCormack, John Donnelly, Mary Cahill, Trevor King. Seated: Vincent McBride, Paul Gallagher.

Omagh Players — A Brief History

With the advent of the swinging sixties the Players continued their endeavours and from their clubrooms above Townsend's Bookie's shop in John Street emanated a series of top class production.

By now Joe Keating had taken on the onerous task of trying to fill the shoes of the late Paddy Bogues as producer and although following in footsteps so illustrious was a daunting one, the show, in the best theatrical tradition, went on.

Productions such as *"Professor Tim"*, *"All the King's Horses"* and *"Paul Twyning"* were produced to join the fondly remembered catalogue of successes enjoyed by the Players. In 1966 Paddy Laird produced a revival of *"Boyd's Shop"* which had proved so memorable for them with their All-Ireland win of the 1940s and which included in its cast the late John McElholm who at 77 years of age once again tackled the role of Rev. Patterson that he had taken over two decades earlier.

Thronged houses greeted each successive production and these continued as the decade waned with Joe Keating once again taking over as producer for the likes of *"Mungo's Mansions"*, *"The Year of the Hiker"* and *"The Far Off Hills"*.

With the 1970s came the "troubles" and all the attendant difficulties which they produced and although *"Ladies in Retirement"* was produced by Paddy Laird in 1971 and was extremely well received, it proved to be the last production by the Players for seven years.

"The Accidental Death Of An Anarchist" — 1997
(l to r): Denise McCartan, Dermot McCormack, Michael Hand.

Omagh Players — A Brief History

In October 1978. however, the boards were trod once again and *"Sailors Beware"* confounded the dire warnings of many by proving to be an outstanding success and poignantly marked the last, and some would say, the finest performance by one of the Players' great stalwarts Kathleen Given.

In 1981 David Fullerton made his debut as producer with *"Night Must Fall"* and its success promoted the Players to once again enter the realm of the Festival circuit and this they did with Paddy Laird's production of *"The Field"*. As always, many hours of hard work and preparation went into the production and these paid off handsomely as a glut of awards were attained culminating in the production being staged at the Ulster Finals in the Opera House in Belfast, an achievement which was recognised when the local council gave the Company a civic reception in honour of their achievement.

More success was to follow with Paddy Laird again holding the reins for the Players' production of *"Sive"* and the retention of the Companies' title in Larne as well as high placings in Enniskillen, Derry, Carrickmore and Portadown saw them once again reach the Ulster Finals, thereby becoming the only group to do so in those successive years.

The Players too were busy in other spheres as they produced under the guidance of Frank Sweeney and Stephen McKenna, a series of highly entertaining and well received revues and pantomimes.

"One Flew Over The Cuckoo's Nest" — 1990.
(l to r): Wendy Rea, Olga Bradshaw (Owen Doody is in background left).

Omagh Players — A Brief History

The Last Ten Years

The last ten years in the history of Omagh Players have been marked by continuous activity. A play has been produced in every year which has then gone on to the Festival circuit—to Ballymoney, Newry, Newtownabbey, Larne, Derry, Enniskillen, Strabane, Ballyshannon, Portadown, Moneyglass, Bangor and Carrickmore.

In addition, the Players have had a summer week in The Hawk's Well Theatre in Sligo with their production of *"Da"* and have appeared on television in *"God's Frontiersmen"*. This last venture gave the Players a view of the professional drama world which left them not a little envious of their vast resources! All of the things which can be so difficult for amateurs — money, costumes, technology, props, rehearsal space — are readily available to a television production team.

The sustained activity of the Players in the years 1984-94 has been made possible by the conscious development of a team approach to production. The director can now rely on a back-up team of experienced workers such as Justin O'Doherty, Vincent McBride, Trevor King, Phemie Glass, Dermot McCormack, Brian Campbell, Pauline Mathers and Michael Caulfield to take care of much of the organisational aspect of the show. The set construction is in the capable hands of Tony McGartland and Pat McAleer and the technical team, Justin O'Doherty, Eddie Fitzpatrick and Michael MacDonald, lend their expertise to lighting and sound. These last two, lighting and sound, have become increasingly important over the past ten years as the Players have included in their repertoire a succession of very challenging plays which demonstrate that the era of the box set is well and truly over. Although local accent imposes some restrictions, a varied programme has been produced which included two American plays — *"The Crucible"* in 1986 and *"One Flew Over The Cuckoo's Nest"* in 1990, directed by Kathleen Hinds, a French play *"Ring Round the Moon"* 1991 directed by Ronnie Moran; and this year's play *"Andorra"* by the Swiss playwright Max Frisch, directed by Kathleen Hinds. Irish plays produced were *"All in Favour Said No"* 1984, *"Da"* 1985, *"The Loves Of Cass Maguire"* 1987, *"Dockers"* 1988, *"The Silver Tassie"* 1992, *"The Chastitute"* 1993 directed by Kathleen Hinds and *"Happy As Larry"* 1989 directed by Ronnie Moran.

In an attempt to broaden their scope the Players also produced three One Act plays in 1987. This venture has not been repeated but it is hoped that in the future the Omagh Players may have the resources in terms of cast and production staff sufficient to vary their programme and to produce more than one play each year. Most of the plays produced recently have large casts which have been beneficial in bringing in new talent to add to the established team of such seasoned Players as Ronnie Moran, Vincent McBride, Dermot McCormack, Trevor King, Patsy McAtee, Paul Gallagher and Pearl Fisher, all of whom are veterans of many productions.

Tyrone County Council — Roads Division

The Roads Division occupied the top floor of the Town Hall before moving into the newly built County Hall in 1963. (l to r): Tony Murnaghan, Gerry McCaughey, Plev Ellis.

The main office:
(l to r): ——, Pat Miller (née Kidd) and engineer Jayantilal Mansukhlal Bakhda (Jay).

CHAPTER 8

The Henderson Family, Omagh

by Uel Henderson

The first record of the Henderson family appears in the papers of The Abercorn Family . . . "The deed made to one William Henderson in the year 1629, grants to him, his heirs and assigns, free liberty power and authority", etc. Later in Canon Gebbie's book "Historical Survey of a Parish 1600–1900", we read of a Robert Henderson in the village of Ardstraw in 1751. The old family burial ground is in the old cemetery at Ardstraw, the last burial was William in November 1875 (born 1817).

William had married Rebecca Gordon of Killygordon. They had seven children. Their first son, also William (born 1848) would eventually move to Omagh and start the Tyrone Foundry, and their third son Robert (born 1852) would purchase lands at Lislimnaghan, Omagh. Today it is owned by his grandson Campbell Henderson.

In 1882, William Henderson purchased property at Glenview on the Kevlin Road from John Samuel Galbraith, formerly the site of the Old Fever Hospital and founded "The Tyrone Foundry". The business opened on 16th December, 1882. Within a short time, threshing machines, churning machines, ploughs, etc. were being manufactured and sold throughout Ireland. Ledgers from 1890 show prices ranging from £29 for threshing machines and churning machines from £11. In 1911, William bought the remaining shares of Omagh Foundry from Thomas James McAdam and Robert Swan. As the dying crafts in the smelting business such as moulding and casting outlived their usefulness, the engineering section prospered and with it the retailing of farm machinery. On the death of William the business passed to his nephew Robert Kerr Henderson at the age of 24.

William Henderson

The Henderson Family

Robert Kerr Henderson (1891–1969)

From an early age R. K. Henderson was deeply involved in the Presbyterian Church, first with Mountjoy Church and later when he moved to live in Omagh, with First Omagh Church. He was a member of the session and elder from 1919 to 1969 and treasurer from 1957 to 1968, and Superintendent of the Sunday School from 1919 to 1958. From 1927, until his death in 1969, Robert Henderson was a Unionist member of Omagh Urban Council and Council Chairman from 1951 to 1960. For over 20 years he was a member of Castlederg Rural Council and a life-long member of the Tyrone Farming Society. He had a long association with the Masonic Order.

His business interests had started in 1915 when he had taken over The Tyrone foundry from his uncle William. The *Tyrone Constitution* of 7th March, 1924 reports, "An interesting property sale carried out during the week was the purchase by Mr. R. K. Henderson of the large residence, yard, offices and extensive gardens lying between High Street and Kevlin Road" *(see cutting opposite)*. In 1925 he transferred the business to High Street. Years later, part of the old Glenview Foundry site was sold to Omagh Council for housing, now Glenview Cottages, and in 1955 Hackett Villas was erected on part of the site. Glenview Terrace remained in the family until the 1960s.

An interesting property sale carried out during this week was the purchase by Mr. R. K. Henderson, Omagh of the large residence in High Street, occupied by Mrs. McCausland and Mr. E. V. Hamilton, solicitor, with large yard, offices and extensive fruit and vegetable gardens lying between High Street and Kevlin Road, the property of the Messrs. Greer and Camus, Strabane. Mr. Henderson subsequently resold four of the smaller gardens to Mr. Frank Crawford and the residence to Mr. W. E. Orr, but retains the large garden, office-houses and yard.

Lord Wakehurst, Governor of Northern Ireland visits Omagh with his wife in the 1950s and is greeted at the Urban District Council Offices by Robert K. Henderson, Chairman.

On the 5th March, 1924 Mr. R. K. Henderson bought, from the Greer estate, 19 High Street, Omagh and the land to the rear which extended to the Kevlin Road, for the sum of £3,400. The same day he sold a portion of the garden to Frank Crawford of Bellevue and a similar piece of land to Fred and Jim Johnston to the rear of W. J. Johnston's shop on the High Street. He sold 19 High Street to W. E. Orr (Solicitor). This property was bought back from a Mrs. H. Cox in 1961. R. K. kept the foundry and a portion of the garden where he built a small house for his sister Ann and her mother. At the end of the day he was in profit.

The Henderson Family

The Queen Mother meets the Omagh Urban District Council in the grounds of Campsie Primary School on her visit to Omagh in 1961. Robert Kerr Henderson also in photo.

By 1931 he had bought premises from the McClay family at John Street, Castlederg and opened a further outlet for the sale of hardware. In 1937 he purchased the newsagency and hardware business in Newtownstewart from his cousin William Ross Henderson. By 1954 the business had become a Limited Company and continued to operate from the premises in High Street. Following the purchase of Charleton's Garage on the Brookmount Road, the business was transferred there with trading starting in November 1982, almost exactly 100 years since William Henderson had started the business at Glenview.

In High Street part of the premises was sold to the road services to become the Foundry Lane car park. Then in 1994 it was decided to cease trading and change direction, and the business became a private investment property company. The site in High Street became the Foundry lane shopping development with 14 shops and offices, a new chapter was under way, but that is for another book.

The Henderson family of Woodvale, Omagh and the Old Methodist Manse, Newtownstewart at the dedication of the Minister's Vestry in First Omagh Presbyterian Church on 25th June, 1977. (l to r): Campbell, Mrs. Helen Henderson, Jayne (grand-daughter), Helen Gillanders and Uel.

Top:
Foundry Lane as it looked in 1960.

Below:
Foundry Lane, High Street, Omagh showing on the left the date of the building of the first half in 1985. There are 14 shops.

The Henderson Family

JAMES MATTHEW HENDERSON, born in July 1889, was the twin son of Robert and Mary Henderson of Woodvale, Lislimnaghan, Omagh, His twin brother, John Kerr, died in March 1890 at 8 months.

James emigrated to Canada and joined the 47th Battalion Canadian Infantry. Within a short time he found himself in Europe. He died in action in France on 25th June, 1917.

The Kerr referred to was from the family in Newtownstewart who had the poet son Robert Kerr killed in the Battle of Jutland while serving on the warship H.M.S. Defence on 31st May, 1916 aged 24.

In Memory of
Lance Corporal JAMES HENDERSON
116447, 47th Bn, Canadian Infantry
(Western Ontario Regiment)
who died age 27 on 25th June, 1917.
Son of Robert and Minnie Henderson
of Woodvale, Omagh, Co. Tyrone, Ireland.
Remembered with honour
Villers Station Cemetery, Villers-Au-Bois

Inscription on the Headstone in France.

The Park, Newtownstewart one time the home of William Ross Henderson.

Main Street, Newtownstewart in the early 20th century showing Henderson's Hardware Shop on the left.

109

CHAPTER 9

Memories of the Past

The North West Agricultural School, Melmount Road, Strabane provided residential courses for females in domestic science, cooking, dairying and poultry. It was set up on 22nd August, 1911.

Also courses of instruction in agriculture were set up by the Department of Agriculture and Technical Institution of Ireland. An agricultural institute for the north west of Ulster was to be set up as a result of a meeting in Derry in 1911. Representatives of the County Commissions of Donegal, Derry and Tyrone,

The school opened in 1914 with 24 places. It closed in 1971 in preference to Loughry.

John David Watson of Dervaghroy, Beragh (circled)
attended the North West Agricultural School in 1912/14.

Memories of the Past

A woman about to get a lift through the flood at the Model School in 1919.

Campsie Canal 1987 — an aerial view of Campsie showing the extent of the severe flood of October 1987 when much damage was done to homes and commercial property.

Memories of the Past

Charlie Mills' shop in Market Street, one of Omagh's finest shop fronts.
It disappeared as a result of the troubles.

Ethne Keenan and Gregory McGale — cousins at Confirmation. Ethne lived above her
parents' butchers shop in Market Street and Gregory, who later worked in the Ulster
Herald, lived above his parents off-licence, McGale & Mullan, also in Market Street.

Boyer's drapers shop, 25 Market Street in the 1920s
(between Keenan's butchers and A. A. Love, Manchester House).

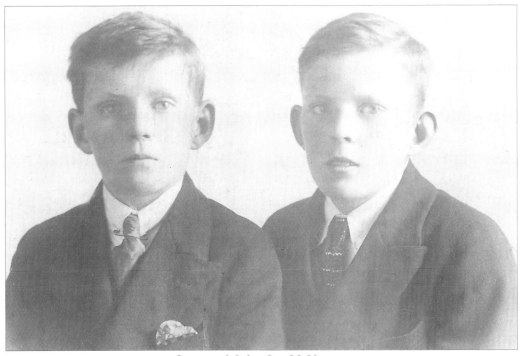

Stan and John Joe McNamee
whose father's Public House was just across the road from Boyer's in Market Street.

Constitutional Club Golf Outing to Baronscourt, Newtownstewart in the 1950s.

Back Row (l to r): Victor Jones (Welfare Officer), Bertie Shaw, Tommy Rutledge, ——, Robin Waterson, Dougie Chambers, Tim Sproule, Murray O'Neile, ——, Bob Nesbitt, John Clements, James Eakin, Walter Steele.

Front Row (l to r): Nat Holmes, Ollie Clements, L. Fryer, Robert Waterson, ——, Dr. James Fulton, Bob Rodgers.

Kerrigan School of Irish Dancing c.1940.

Back Row (l to r): Linus Nugent, Myles Corry, Michael McGrath, Dan Murray, Sean Donnelly, Billy Vaughan, Jackie Kelly.
Middle Row (l to r): Seamus Gormley, Liam McCusker, Gerard Mulvey, Irvine Nugent, Eugene McCanny, Ray McCann, Patsy Donnelly.
Front Row (l to r): Michael Vaughan, Jim Murphy, Eugene Connolly, ——, ——, Frank McGirr, Jackie Hunter, Gerard McCann.

Sadie Devlin of "St. Anne's", 4 Killyclogher Road doing her shopping and just taking a few minutes with George Anderson of Anderson Brothers to discuss the affairs of the town in 1944.

Culmore School in the mid-Thirties — Pupils, Teachers.

Mr. Patrick Friel (Principal), Miss Mary McCrossan (Assistant), Miss Agnes Mossey (Assistant). Included are members of the school choir (trained by Mr. P Friel) which won the two trophies (for Unison and Harmonised Choir) at the Tyrone Feis that year.

Back Row (l to r): Patrick Friel (D), Rose ——, May Knox (McNamee), Katy Maynes (Duffy), Nanette Friel (D) (Pickhaver), Christina Friel (Passmore), Kitty Johnston, Agnes McGale (D).

Middle Row (l to r): Miss Mary McCrossan, Kathleen Winters, Bridie Kennedy (Meyler), Arthur McGale, Mena Kearney (D) (McGirr), Rita Kearns, Maureen McAleer, Eileen McAleer, Sheila Daly, Rose Conway (Quinn), Phillip McGlynn (dec.), Miss Agnes Mossey.

Front Row (l to r): Frankie Turbitt, Mary Friel (McMahon), Ellie Conway, Jackie Kennedy, The Master, Eileen Kearney (Carney), Brian Friel (the Playwright), Mena Teague, Nance Friel (Stewart), Annie Mullan.   Kneeling: (l to r): Claire Friel (Fullerton), Sonny (Ted) Pritchard, Mary Keaveney (Livingstone).

Photograph courtesy of Chris Passmore

117

Memories of the Past

Gas Managers' Conference at Coleraine in 1965. Tom Hastings (centre in light jacket) was Omagh's Manager for 30 years. He came in the early 1940s as engineering manager and died in 1974.

An exhibition of gas products (just after the war) in J. B. Anderson's corner window. Note the prices. No reminder of Omagh's Gasworks which was built in the 1850s now exists.

Memories of the Past

Thomas Scarffe and his wife outside the gates of Mount Pleasant, Coneywarren in 1938.

The staff of Thomas Scarffe & Son also in 1938.

Canon Charles Cullimore outside the Rectory in Campsie in the 1940s.
The house was built in the mid 19th century by Seaton F. Milligan, M.R.I.A., father of Alice the well known writer, poet and Gaelic League sympathiser. She was born in Gortmore but lived for a period in this house before going on her travels. She returned in later life and lived for a period in the Old Rectory in Mountfield. She died at Cullion, Lislap and is buried in Drumragh Old Graveyard.   Ref. *"Tombstones of the Omey" by Wm. McGrew.*

Memories of the Past

Top:
Alice L. Milligan in her later years.

Bottom:
Her grave at Drumragh in front of the family grave. A wreath is laid each Easter Sunday by the local Republican Club.

Born September 1866, died April 1953.

Memories of the Past

Y.M.C.A. Tennis Club in the 1940s with a serviceman looking on.
Stand (l to r): Scottish Soldier, ——, Isobel Anderson, — Armstrong, Herbie McComiskey, Ira Love.
Sitting (l to r); Jean Hopper, Denise White, Gretta Carson, ——, Betty Adams.

Swimmers at the Leap in the 1940s.
(l to r): Ira Love, Dr. Brendan Kelly, Jim Coulter, Wilmer Mitchell.

More Education Staff.
Lily Johnston and Mabel McCarter.

Education Staff after the war.
(l to r): Harold McCauley, Violet Wilton, Andy Gibson (County
Education Officer).

Memories of the Past

POSTERS ADVERTISING PROPERTY FOR SALE
Selling property hasn't changed much over the years . . . only the price has gone up somewhat!

Memories of the Past

A David Brown tractor traversing the flood waters at the Dublin Road corner in 1951.

The same flood water with a boat for transport.

Memories of the Past

Omagh Show 1949. Ollie Clements, his ambulance and four members of the Red Cross. Note the Nissan Huts in the background; they were used by the Americans during the war.

Charlie Anderson feeding chickens in a field on the Old Mountfield Road where he built a bungalow "Sunnycrest" in the 1950s. The field behind him contains the 26 houses of Sunnycrest Gardens today. The house in the background (left) was McCartney's.

Memories of the Past

Motor Cycle enthusiasts on the Old Mountfield Road about to go for a run in the country in the 1950s.

An early Tyrone car (JI 270) on the Belfast to Larne run in the 1950s.

Photo: Father Donal B. Gillespie

Father Denis Torney (Bubbles) gives his blessing to his father Harry Torney after being newly ordained in St. Mary's Church, Killyclogher on 11th February, 1952, while his mother and the midwife who delivered him look on. On the right is Norah Torney, (widow of Billy) and Harry Junior with his wife Imelda. The boy in the background is the next Harry Torney.

St. Columba's Badminton Club Outing to Donegal on Whit Monday 1954.

Back Row (l to r): Norman Craig, Harry Graham, Bill Roulston, Charlie Snell.

Third Row (l to r): Charlie Allen, Ethel Caldwell (née Stewart), Rene Johnston, Peggy Crawford (née Caldwell), Margaret McLean (née Pyne), Olive Allen (née Ingram), Sgt. Gamble.

Second Row (l to r): Billy Burton, Julie Burton (née Allen), Aileen Pollard (née Lee), Fred McCluskey, Mrs. Gamble, Mrs. Roulston (née Emo), Roy Barton, Noel Mitchell.

Front Row (l to r): Billy Caldwell, Ruth Kissinger (née Cockburn), Isobel Anderson, Gladys Potts, Violet Wilton, Sarah Snell, Thelma Barton, George Thompson.

CHAPTER 10

The Troubles
and the events following Sat., 15th August, 1998

In the late 1960s the Civil Rights Movement became active and many confrontations with the R.U.C. took place. As a result the 'Troubles' were ignited and developed into a situation that involved the British Army and the Paramilitaries being in constant conflict for 30 years.

Many buildings were destroyed by explosives and fire while over 3,000 citizens were killed in explosions and shootings over the period.

Omagh had 46 bombings that caused varying degrees of destruction and death.

Premises damaged in Market Street following a bomb outside the offices of Northern Ireland Electricity. Inset: McCaul's Footwear destroyed in the same bomb.

The Troubles and the events following Saturday, 15th August, 1998

Knock-na-Moe Castle Hotel was frequently bombed both inside and out.
This small bomb was in a car parked outside the front doors.

The night Omagh burned — 9th February, 1974. A view of High Street showing
Lyons paint shop on fire. The same night, Bloomfield's draper shop, Black's furniture
store and Woolworths in Market Street were all destroyed by fire.

The Troubles and the events following Saturday, 15th August, 1998

After several bombings J.B. Anderson's eventually succumbed to incendiary devices in May 1977. It was re-built only to be destroyed again on the 15th August, 1998.

Photography: Marie O'Neill

Clement's building which had stood at the Dublin Road corner since 1905 was destroyed by bombs from both sides especially the bomb in Boyd's entry on the 12th January 1974. As a result the building had to be demolished. Ref. Vol. 9 "Images of Omagh"

Saturday, 15th August, 1998

The cease fire was months old and the population was enjoying the summer weather. The Real or Dissident IRA were bombing Ulster towns on a regular basis to show their disagreement with the cease fire. They bombed Portadown, Banbridge and Moira for example, but never for one minute did the people of Omagh feel that they would be a target.

But on Saturday, 15th August, 1998, a car bomb was left outside a draper's shop in Market Street — the bombers' warning was for a bomb near the Courthouse and the public was ushered down the street to where the bomb was sited. When the bomb exploded at 3.10 p.m. the results were devastating with 31 dead and hundreds seriously injured.

The wounds remain for the bereaved and the injured have to suffer the loss of limbs and sight with permanent injuries both physical and psychological for the rest of their lives.

The legal aspects of the case continue with two men charged with the bombing and making the bomb.

A memorial to the dead has been erected on Drumragh Avenue near the bomb site.

Spiller's Place being demolished in September 1972 — not as a result of a bomb but to make way for the new library.   Photo: Marie O'Neill

After Saturday, 15th August, 1998

The car carrying the bomb photographed minutes before the explosion, taken by one of the Spanish children from the Buncrana Summer School who were visiting Omagh that day. The camera was found in the rubble.

An aerial view of the bomb site shortly after the explosion.

After Saturday, 15th August, 1998

1.20 p.m. on Saturday, 22nd August, 1998 — some of the thousands walking along Bridge Street on their way to the Memorial Service in High Street. The Service was televised all over the world.

Sent from all over the world, masses of flowers, later preserved in floral art form and given to the bereaved. The person in the photo is architect Keith Gilmour (a native of Omagh) who helped in the re-building of Market Street.

After Saturday, 15th August, 1998

The Remembrance Garden on the site of the Kozy Corner Bar which was used on the First Anniversary by those who wished to lay flowers.

Memorial Services have been held each year since the 15th August, 1998 at the temporary Memorial Garden in Drumragh Avenue. Margaret Mitchell is singing on 15th August, 2003. On the extreme right is Mr. Paddy McLoone.

After Saturday, 15th August, 1998

The 1st July, 1999 — Omagh District Lodges gather at the Orange Hall for a Service and parade to remember the 5,000 or more Ulstermen who died on the first day of the Battle of the Somme. This year they were remembering as well those who died in the Omagh Bomb almost one year ago. Ivan Cooper is discussing affairs with the Rev. Harry Cairns before the commencement of the parade.

At the bomb site the parade halts for a short service conducted by Wilfred Breen.

After Saturday, 15th August, 1998

The Memorial to the victims of the Omagh Bomb on Drumragh Avenue as it is at present. A final decision has yet to be made on the permanent Memorial of Remembrance.

An inscription is in English, Spanish and Irish.

The Last Ten Years

Since the cease fire, negotiations with the on and off Northern Ireland Assembly have moved on with the development of the economics of the country and the cutting back of all things military — the membership of the R.U.C. is reduced and the name changed to the Police Service of Northern Ireland. The numbers of the military are also being reduced and garrisons across the province outback are closed.

Omagh suffered on two fronts with the closure of both its barracks. Lisanelly families left in the summer of 2006 while the soldiers of the K.O.S.Bs left in September 2006. The 4th Battalion The Royal Irish Regiment stationed in Omagh were stood down on 31st July, 2007 and St. Lucia Barracks officially closed.

The future of these centre-of-town properties has yet to be decided.

The 4th Battalion (R.I.R.) paraded for the final time before the Queen at a commemorative event at Balmoral Showgrounds, Belfast on Friday, 6th October, 2006 marking the end of operational duties in Northern Ireland and the conclusion of 36 years loyal service.

At the ceremony the Queen presented the Conspicuous Gallantry Cross to a female Corporal of the Regiment.

274 serving and ex-serving personnel were lost to terrorist action in Northern Ireland.

The original entrance to St. Lucia Barracks via Barrack Lane in 1900. The married quarters were on the left of photograph where the new P.S.N.I. regional headquarters is built.

The Pipes and Drums of the Ulster Defence Regiment playing at a Fête in the Showgrounds in 1994.

The shooting range at Lislap used during World War II and by the 'B' Specials, the U.D.R. and the army up until recently.

A common sight in Omagh during the troubles — the armed soldier in combat gear, transported by army Land Rover.

The sound of helicopters filled the Omagh sky on a day and night basis. This Wessex at St. Lucia was commonly used to transfer troops — the Gazelle, Lynx, Puma and Chinook were also to be seen in the skies above the town.

The Last Ten Years

Following 9/11 the Twin Towers Disaster in New York, Omagh paid its respect to the dead in a Remembrance Service at the Ulster-American Folk Park — "Across The Ocean". Margaret Mitchell is seen singing.

Members of the Rotary Club of Omagh on a tour of St. Lucia Barracks in May 2003, conducted by Jack Dunlop, Curator of the Enniskillen Military Museum.

The Last Ten Years

Drumhead Service in Omagh Showgrounds in 1959 to dedicate new Legion Standard.
(l to r): Tommy McFarland (Secretary), Vincent Rodgers (Chief Standard Bearer), Bobby
McFarland (Chairman). Seated is Major Tom 'Roguey' Maguire (President).

Legion members at the opening of the new Legion premises at Campsie Road in 1955.
Back Row (l to r): Jim Gregg, Alston Ward, George Carmichael, Charles McKeown, Owen
Duffy, Jack Simpson, Dick Byrne, Jim McMorris, Jim Elliott, Cyril Baillie,
Capt. C. N. M. Rountree, Sammy Graham, Ivan Allen, Hugh Campbell,
Kathleen Twist, Florrie Elliott, Ossie McKelvey.
Middle Row (l to r): Celene Coyle, Vincent Rodgers, Mrs. Rodgers, Eileen Byrne, Nan Leitch,
Amy Ward, Ruby Carmichael.
Front Row (l to r): Willie McFarland, Brian Coyle, Christie Leitch, George McClelland, Bob Martin.

The Regimental Association of the Ulster Defence Regiment (County West Tyrone Committee) being led by the Regimental Band to the Annual Commemoration Service of Thanksgiving and Remembrance in St. Columba's Parish Church, Omagh on Sunday, 12th June, 2005. The Queen's Colour 6th (County Tyrone) Battalion and the Regimental Colour 6th (County Tyrone) Battalion were deposited in this church on 11th December, 1994.

Beating Retreat

*The Commanding Officer, Lieutenant Colonel J. V. K. Harris
and all Ranks
4th Battalion The Royal Irish Regiment
request the pleasure of your company
at a Beating Retreat and refreshments
to be held at St Lucia Barracks, Omagh
on Tuesday, 10th September 2002
from 7.00pm to 9.30pm*

The Ceremony of Beating Retreat

The Ceremony of Beating Retreat dates from the very early days of the British Army. It is believed to have originated in those days when towns and cities were huddled round the castle walls for protection, and was the signal for the soldiers to return to the security of the castle before the raising of the drawbridge for the night.

It is recorded that during the wars in the reign of King William III, all soldiers were billeted in taverns or in private homes and the Orderly Officer with the drums paraded through the streets to warn the soldiers to return to their billets at curfew time. First the buglers sounded the First Post, then the drummers beat Tattoo for half an hour, culminating in the sounding of the Last Post. As this was before the introduction of "time, gentlemen please", it also served as a signal for tavern keepers to turn off the taps, i.e. Taptoe, a word which the troops soon turned into Tattoo.

The system of billeting eventually fell into disuse, but the ceremony of beating retreat has been retained until the present, as a reminder of this ancient custom.

The Band of the Royal Irish Regiment

The Band of the Royal Irish Regiment was formed in 1993 by the amalgamation of the Regimental Bands of the 1st and 2nd Battalions of the Royal Irish Regiment. The band has been at St. Patrick's Ballymena since 1994. It has been constantly in demand at many Regimental and public events. Providing musical support at Royal occasions and Government events also forms part of the Band's official duties. Significant events since 1993 have included performances at the British Embassy in Washington DC., The Royal Tournament, The Festival of Remembrance at the Royal Albert Hall, The Edinburgh Tattoo and tours of Germany, Romania and Canada.

Lisanelly — the interior of St. Patrick's Garrison Church.
Window left — dedicated to the Queen's Lancashire Regiment.
Window right — dedicated to the Queen's Dragoon Guards.

The entrance to Lisanelly Barracks on the Gortin Road in September 2006 when the K.O.S.Bs departed.

Lieutenant Colonel R Jefferies

and the Officers of the

1ˢᵗ Battalion The King's Own Scottish Borderers

request the pleasure of

at *a Regimental Cocktail Party*
on *Wednesday 29th June 2005*

Dress: Suits
6.30 for 7 pm.

A member of the regiment dances the Highland Fling to the pipes and drums of the regiment. This may have been their last performance in public in Omagh.

The last appearance of the Pipes and Drums of the Royal Irish Regiment at a Remembrance Sunday Service in Omagh on 13th November, 2005.

The Last Ten Years

Daryl Simpson visits First Omagh Presbyterian Church on Christmas Eve 2006 to sing to the congregation. It was Daryl who got the local community leaders together after the Omagh Bomb to form the Omagh Community Youth Choir. He is now singing with the Celtic Tenors. Also in the photograph are Margaret Mitchell, Jean Murray (organist) and Rev. John F. Murdoch.

Jean Murray at the console of the recently restored pipe organ of First Omagh Presbyterian Church.

CHAPTER 11

The Tyrone and Fermanagh Hospital

The large hospital complex was built round the original lunatic asylum of 1847–53 by William Farrell. Farrell's asylum, one of the second series erected by the Irish Board of Works at a cost of £35,000, is a daunting three-storey range in an oppressive institutional Elizabethan style, seventy-two window bays long. Symmetrical, though broken by varied projections with grouped brick chimney stacks and massive square stair-towers with octagonal cupoles exactly like those on Wilkinson's Workhouses. In 1863, extensive additions were made by George Boyd, and in 1895–9 a new County Infirmary was built by C. A. Owen who also designed the Catholic and Protestant chapels of 1901 and 1903.

Ref. "North West Ulster" by Alistair Rowan

The impressive entrance to the hospital which was once surrounded by a high wall with a narrow entrance. Ref. Vol. 7 "Images of Omagh" pages 64 and 83 and also "The T & F, A Chronological History" by Robert McKinley.

The Tyrone and Fermanagh Hospital

Dr. Francis John West, M.D., M.R.C.S.E. was the first Resident Medical Superintendent of the Institution. The hospital opened for the reception of patients on 2nd May, 1853 and the complete Minutes of all meetings of the Board of Governors and Guardians are to be found in a bound collection in the hospital office, giving its history from its inception. Dr. F. J. West was related to the Herdmans of Sion Mills. He died in service on 23rd October, 1880. There is a memorial window to his life and work in St. Columba's Parish Church, Omagh.

Headstone in Edenderry Church of Ireland graveyard where he is buried, reads: "In Memory of Francis John West, M.D., born 16th December, 1811, died 23rd October, 1880".

"Strathdene" the residence of the R.M.S., situated at the entrance end of the hospital grounds — now used as office accommodation.

The Tyrone and Fermanagh Hospital

A full view of the hospital frontage as it looks today.

An aerial view from the front gives an impression of the enormity of the hospital site and its various units. At the rear, Pine and Larch, to the left of the river and the Villas to the right. In the middle the main original block from the gate lodge to Strathdene; while in the front close to Cranny Bridge are the blocks originally built as nurses' homes but now occupy a variety of medical out-patients and offices.

Tyrone and Fermanagh Mental Hosital — Senior Officers and Male Staff 1945.

Back Row (l to r):   J. Coyle, J. McManus, P Kelly, A. Smith, J. Thompson, G. Boyle, J. Flanagan, W. Ross, J. Allen, S. Donaghy, C. Ross, R. Duncan.

Third Row (l to r):   P. Breen, J. McMichael, J. O'Donnell, P. McSwiggan, L. Porter, H. McSwiggan, A. McAleer, A. Greer, F. Scullion, M. McCormick, J. McLean, T. Ewing.

Second Row (l to r):   R. Ewing, T. Bell, B. Wilkinson, F. Lilley, J. Kyle, F. Coyle, C. Shannon, J. McCanny, P. Mullan, T. Coyle, T. Baker, W. Steele, W. Duncan, J. Maguire, H. Johnston, E. Moss, G. Maguire.

Front Row (l to r):   Wm. Ballantine, J. Ingram, O. L. Walsh, David Barbour, Miss I. Guy, Dr. W. Kelly, Dr. M. Roche, Dr. J. Moore Johnston, Dr. J. E. Herbert, Miss Robb, Miss Marion Mitchell, J. McConkey, Mrs. M. McFarland, H. Ronaldson, F. Patterson.

153

The Tyrone and Fermanagh Hospital

The centre of the main block that once housed the doctors' quarters, the board-room and main offices. Today it houses the offices of the Sperrin Lakeland Trust.

Dr. John Patrick, M.B., for 20 years R.M.S. at the T. & F. Hospital and Prof. Edward Thompson, Consultant Surgeon at the Tyrone County Hospital front entrance in the 1920s.

JOHN PATRICK, M.B.
FOR 20 YEARS R.M.S. OMAGH MENTAL HOSPITAL
BORN CARRICKFERGUS 11TH AUG. 1869
DIED 5TH AUG. 1933.

Dr. Patrick's grave at Edenderry Parish Church.

The gate lodge at the T. & F. Hospital — built in 1854.

The front hall of the main entrance block.

The Catholic Chapel (built in 1901) which is at the back of the main block. It seats 300 and has an average attendance at Mass on Sunday mornings of about 70.

The interior of the Catholic Chapel.

The Protestant Church (built in 1903) just inside the main gate.

The interior of the Protestant Church which was used up until recently by Church of Ireland, Presbyterian and Methodists in rotation. Now closed.

The Tyrone and Fermanagh Hospital

Some well known staff who attended the Retirement Presentation of the hospital secretary James Henderson on 31st August, 1990.
(l to r): J. Gormley, Brendan Colgan (Finance), James Henderson, Miss Pat Donald (Nursing Staff), John Armstrong (Social Services), Mr. T. J. Wilmot, F.R.C.S. (Chairman Hospital Committee).

Robert McKinley giving a lecture on the hospital's history to visitors in the Protestant Church (1995). He was on the management staff for over 32 years.

The Tyrone and Fermanagh Hospital

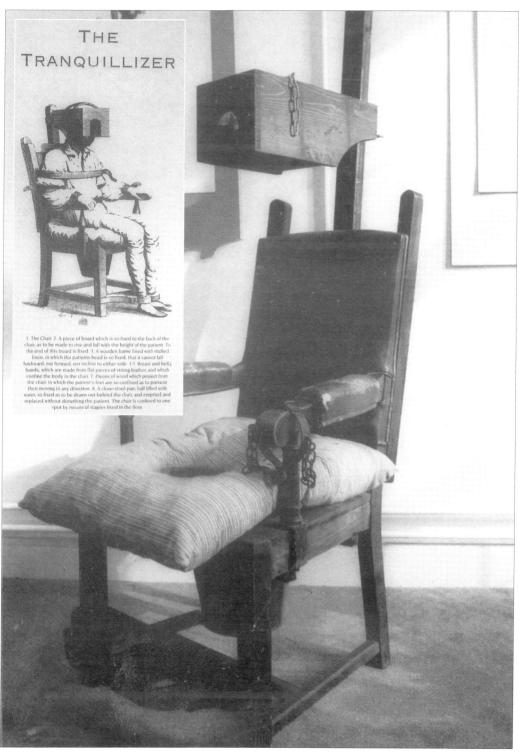

THE
TRANQUILLIZER

1. The Chair. 2. A piece of board which is so fixed to the back of the chair, as to be made to rise and fall with the height of the patient. To the end of this board is fixed. 3. A wooden frame lined with stuffed linen, in which the patients head is so fixed, that it cannot fall backward, nor forward, nor incline to either side. 4.5. Breast and belly bands, which are made from flat pieces of strong leather, and which confine the body in the chair. 7. Pieces of wood which project from the chair, in which the patient's feet are so confined as to prevent their moving in any direction. 8. A close-stool-pan, half filled with water, so fixed as to be drawn out behind the chair, and emptied and replaced without disturbing the patient. The chair is confined to one spot by means of staples fixed in the floor.

A restrainer chair with fittings which was used to treat difficult patients in the days before the drugs we have today. Inset: A description on how the chair was to be used.

The Tyrone and Fermanagh Hospital

In 1954 Oliver A. Evans, S.R.N., R.M.N., was appointed to the position of Chief Male Nurse from a short list of seven.

At that time the number of in-patients was 992 and still rising.

Sadly Mr. Evans' successful career, was cut short by his sudden death in 1971, aged 55.

The opening of the new clinic on the Sixmilecross Road in 1955
by Lady Wakehurst, wife of the Governor of Northern Ireland.
(l to r): ——, Norman Wilson, Chairman of the T. & F. Management
Committee, Lady Wakehurst, Oliver Evans (Chief Male Nurse).
Nurses (from left): Joe Young, ——, Joe Dunn, Edward Orr, Robert Duncan, Emerson
McCarron, Arthur Moffitt, Joe O'Donnell.

The Tyrone and Fermanagh Hospital

Opening of new clinic in 1955 by Lady Wakehurst.
(l to r): ——, Norman Wilson, Cissie Quinn, Lady Wakehurst, Oliver A. Evans talking to (l to r) Bob Nixon, Tom Bell, Jimmy Thompson, Leslie Reynolds.

Presentation of first colour television in 1970s.
(l to r): Dr. Tom Haran, Paddy Sweeney, Cissie Quinn, John Maguire, Gerry Hutchinson, Bobby Jameson, Mickey McCormick, Matron Mellor.

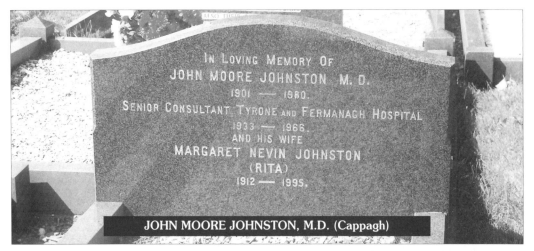

JOHN MOORE JOHNSTON, M.D. (Cappagh)

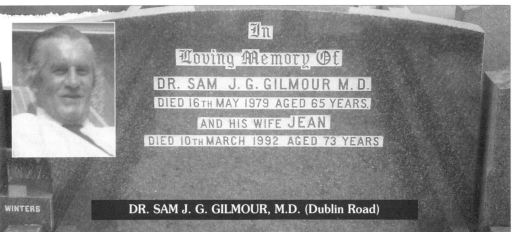

DR. SAM J. G. GILMOUR, M.D. (Dublin Road)

DR. TOM HARAN (Killyclogher)

The final resting places of three of the T. & F's best remembered Consultants of the last generation. They looked after the hospital when the patient population was at its highest. In the early 1960s there were 1,100 patients and 750 staff — Omagh's largest employer.

The Tyrone and Fermanagh Hospital

Sketch by Mr. John Wright.

CRANNY CHURCH HUT

PARISH OF EDENDERRY

Cranny Church Hut was built in 1953, the first Service being held on Christmas Day, since then Holy Communion Services have been held there on the third Sunday of every month. A Sunday School was started in January 1954.

This building was erected to meet the needs of the people living in the vicinity of the Tyrone and Fermanagh Hospital, who are unable to attend the Parish Church, which is almost in the south-west corner of the parish. As there was no place in that district where services could be held and no funds to erect a large building, and as the whole idea was in the nature of an experiment, it was felt that, as the Scottish proverb says, "Sma' fish are better than name", and so a very small corrugated iron building (8 feet by 20 feet) was erected, but, from the start, this has proved to be too small. The cost of this building having been completely cleared off, it has been decided to put up a larger building, also of corrugated iron, in which other Services and meetings may be held and where there may be better accommodation for the Sunday School, which is carrying on under great difficulties. It is to help towards the cost of the new building that this calendar has been produced, and we are very grateful to all the subscribers, collectors and, not least of all, the advertisers, for their ready and generous help.

Committee
Messrs: F. Coyle, J. Faulkner, T. Ewing,
Mrs. C. McKelvey, Mrs. H. Armstrong, Mrs. Moffitt, Mrs. P. McCrory and Miss C. McCreery

Hon. Secretary and Treasurer
Mr. F. Coyle, 5 Cranny Terrace, Omagh

Sunday School Teachers
Mr. John McKelvey, The Misses F. Ewing and B. McCrory

From a Parish Calendar produced in 1956 to raise funds for a new building. No building exists today.

CHAPTER 12

Ulster–American Folk Park

The Ulster–American Folk Park celebrated 30 years in 2006 and it is now one of the six top public attractions in Northern ireland with its unique blend of entertainment centred round the emigration of Ulstermen and women to the U.S.A. Enactments of a frontier wedding to the now ever popular Annual Appalachian Bluegrass Music Festival which draws the best in that kind of music to perform in an out of the Park's exhibits and in the larger marque.

Terry Patterson interviews Rotarian John Gilmour on the occasion of the Park's Silver Jubilee. John is a director of the Park and of M.A.G.N.I.

Rotarian John Gilmour with Anthea Turner and Gordon Kennedy (BBC) when the 24th National Lottery Draw came to the Folk Park on 29th April, 1995.

Director reflects on 'amazing' growth of the Park

by Terry Patterson

From little acorns, large trees grow. Never did the unfailing proverb find a more appropriate use than to describe the amazing development of the Ulster-American Folk Park.

Established in 1968 as a small National Trust facility focused on the Mellon Homestead and the Camphill Viewpoint, it had, by 1976, become a 20-acre site and was renamed the Ulster–American Folk Park. It is currently an all-embracing and superb 80-acre tourist and visitor attraction known throughout the world.

And it now has a burgeoning 130,000 visitors a year, compared to the 250 or so souls who annually took an inquiring or curious glance at the restored Camphill cottage 33 years ago.

The Park's astonishing growth mirrors the miraculous achievements of its benefactors the Mellon family itself, according to its director, John Gilmour who is equally surprised to find he is still there 23 years after he should have returned to teaching at Omagh Academy.

Just three weeks after the Folk Park, the brain-child of Eric Montgomery, a retired Stormont information officer, officially opened in July 1976, John, now 52, was seconded to it by the Western Education and Library Board for what was to have been a two-year stint as education officer.

James Mellon (Chairman of the Ulster Scots Trust)
addressing guests on the occasion of the Park's 25th Anniversary Celebrations.

Ulster–American Folk Park

Instead, he stayed on and succeeded Mr. Montgomery, who had initially run the Folk Park part-time with a six-strong staff, in 1992, having four years earlier been named head of museum services.

"Great credit is due to Eric for founding, on his retirement, what is now a very successful modern-day museum. He did so in collaboration with Dr. Matthew Mellon, a great-grandson of the original emigrant, Thomas Mellon," explained Mr. Gilmour. "I marvel greatly at what the Mellon family achieved. Thomas, who became a judge, founded the family banking empire in Pittsburg, Pennsylvania and the bank now dominates the city skyline.

"I have seen with my own eyes the green neon lettering topping two magnificent Mellon skyscrapers and when I do I reflect on a small thatched cottage located near Omagh that Thomas left as a five-year old in 1818. Sadly, Matthew Mellon died in 1993 and has been succeeded by his son, James Mellon, as President of the Scotch-Irish Trust."

Mr. Gilmour outlined how Mr. Montgomery had procured funding for the original Mellon homestead from the family, and how he had proceeded to set up a trust that later funded the purchase of additional land on which the modern visitors centre at the Folk Park was built.

"When I arrived in 1976, Eric Montgomery was running the museum with an administrator seconded from the Forestry Service — Jack Devenney — while the

The Indian encampment — resting during the
U.S. Independence Celebrations on 6th July, 2003.

166

Ulster–American Folk Park

late Pat McHugh ran the day-to-day operations. My first problem was to secure staff to meet visitors, and that led to the recruitment of a part-time guide team to welcome the public and to work with the schools," revealed John.

"Eric still takes a tremendous interest in the park and visits frequently."

A native of Omagh, John Gilmour was educated at the local Academy and Queen's University, Belfast, where he gained a history degree. He then secured an M.A. Masters from the University of Ulster, Coleraine campus.

'Option'

"I had the option to return to teaching in 1978, but the Folk Park's education officer post was made permanent and I decided to stay with it. For the next 10 years I developed a series of educational programmes for schools, young people and mature learners," disclosed John.

"Museums are not just about schoolchildren learning, but also about providing all visitors with entertaining and enjoyable learning experiences. There was a strong emphasis on education of the Folk Park from the outset, but I was also charged with helping to market and develop it in a bid to attract as many visitors as possible.

"By 1988 my job had grown significantly and I was engaged in marketing, promotion, major events and fundraising. Tony Nicholl had already been brought in as administrator and then Evelyn Cardwell was appointed as education officer in succession to me."

The British Red Coats involved in the
U.S. Independence Celebrations on 6th July, 2003.

Ulster–American Folk Park

The rapid expansion of the 1980s, notably in visitor numbers and programming also pointed up the need for specialist staff. People with financial administrative and curatorial skills were urgently needed, as John described.

"Denis MacNeice had come to see the Park as more of a museum, a place to preserve original buildings, house collections of objects, and place emphasis on research, education, resources and teaching," he said. "A museum is a major attraction and we never underestimated that, and thus the complex structure of a modern business began to take shape. Everyone has been surprised at just how successful we have become in our location.

"But there have been one or two difficult years, not least the town centre bombing which had a devastating effect on the local area, and the foot-and-mouth epidemic, which hopefully, we have seen off.

Other factors which impact on visitor numbers include Drumcree, the exchange rate, and the price of fuel. Each year brings its own set of circumstances and problems, and none goes smoothly enough to make me complacent.

"However, I am sufficiently optimistic as to believe we are on target to reach the magical 150,000 annual visitor figure in mid-decade with the current product, and the advent of M.A.G.N.I. (Museums and Galleries Northern Ireland) in 1998 has been a massive boost."

The Mellon House round which the whole park was erected.
Shown is Holly Hill (staff) with visiting pupils in period costume.

Aiming to be leading 'museum of emigration'

TO EVOLVE as an unrivalled Museum of Emigration is the ambitious long-term plan for the Ulster–American Folk Park, it has been revealed.

Folk Park director, John Gilmour, said: "Currently we depict emigration from Ulster to the USA over the 18th and 19th centuries, but we are currently taking steps to expand our brief by looking at emigration from all parts of Ireland to all parts of the world.

"For example, we want to study emigration to Australia and South Africa, and, significantly, to mainland Britain, which is all too often overlooked. This departure will bring a major change to our exhibition galleries and to how we interpret the many individual stories of the thousands who left these shores over a 400-year period."

The museum's present emigration package is largely focused on the Ship and Dockside Gallery, launched in the late 1980s thanks to the vision of former director, Denis MacNeice.

"That exhibit is a lasting tribute to Denis, and was a huge milestone in the life of the Folk Park," conceded Mr. Gilmour. "It boosted visitor numbers from around 50,000 to 80,000 and saw them creep past the 100,000 mark. "The ship and Ulster and American streets alongside fired the imagination of visitors who gained a clearer understanding of the hardships endured during an Atlantic crossing that could last anything from seven to 12 weeks.

The forge — it is always popular with the visitors.

Ulster–American Folk Park

"Opening the emigrants' exhibition in 1994, our first major indoor project, supplied the historical background to complement the outdoor site. More recently the Centre for Migration Studies came to fruition and added another resource for researchers of all ages.

"If we can successfully combine the exhibits and research materials to tell the story of the Irish emigrant, and recount his/her personal history and contribution to life in another part of the world, that will make the Ulster–American Folk Park a key player both in the tourist industry and in education and scholarship."

Museum 'thriving and expanding'

The Ulster–American Folk Park has a thriving and expanding CV, according to its director, John Gilmour.

Speaking of the museum's success, Mr. Gilmour said the record of achievement over the past 25 years was a phenomenal one.

He went on: "Every facet of the park is an achievement, from the Dockside Gallery to the ongoing development of historic exhibits, both indoors and out. We opened two original houses last year that had been brought over from America in the latest stage of our New World project.

The ladies are pulling and stooking flax.
(l to r): Dorothy Fulton, Helen McDowell and Olive Breslin.

Ulster–American Folk Park

"The Samuel Fulton [he emigrated from Ramelton, Co. Donegal in the late 18th Century] stone house from near Donegal Springs in Pennsylvania, for which we received Heritage Lottery Funding, and the log house, that had been storage for a number of years, were unveiled to the public.

"Both had been numbered brick by brick, log by log, dismantled, transported and re-erected. And we obtained a very special collection of early 19th century Pennsylvania furnishings, and opened the late 18th century Tullyallen Mass House."

But the Folk Park director said it was not only exhibits that contributed to the growing CV, but a raft of special events, too.

"We stage the annual Appalachian and Bluegrass Music Festival," said Mr. Gilmour. "This year's event is the tenth anniversary one and is a three-day programme from September 7th to 9th.

"And the Park's Hallowe'en Festival is now such that, after 15 years, we no longer need to advertise it. The annual rituals, customs and amusements of Halloween as it was celebrated in Ireland and rural Pennsylvania and Virginia have become so popular that admission is by ticket only, and bookings start as the previous year's ends.

"Among other attractions we mount there is the July 4th Independence Day programme launched in the late 1980s. It began as an experiment to gauge appeal and we were pleasantly surprised that it captured so many people's imaginations. It is now an annual occasion.

"It proved people do value links and family connections with the USA, and will continue to provide them."

The Park in winter.

The Campbell House under construction. It was removed from Aghalane, Plumbridge.

The Emigrant Ship. A scene showing a family about to embark for the New World. One of the most popular exhibits.

Ulster–American Folk Park

A letter from America — the receiver cannot read so the lady is reading the letter to him with everyone else listening on and responding with appropriate remarks. (l to r): Paddy Montague, Roberta Maxwell, Barry Woods, Patrick O'Kane and Thelma Loane.

The 'American Wake' when the family gather together to bid a sad farewell to the departing emigrant. (l to r): Marion Russell, Peter Sammons and Patrick O'Kane.

The Frontier Wedding — waiting for the horse-driven vehicle to arrive with the bride.

The preacher holding forth to the prospective groom before entering the house to meet his bride. (l to r): Paul Bilson, Nancy Elkin, Walter McFarlane, Patrick O'Kane, Peter Sammons and Richard Hurst.

Ulster–American Folk Park

The American Civil War Re-enactment — showing both Confederate and Union troops marching on Omagh's Tourist Office to promote the 4th July celebrations led by Cameron Robinson.

The members of the Ulster–American Folk Park occasionally come to town. This group is performing the Irish Classical Mummers play outside the Tourist Information Office in December 2001.
(l to r): Trevor Miskelly, Richard Hurst, Susan Green, Peter Sammons and Patrick O'Kane.

Ulster–American Folk Park

The Ulster–American Folk Park thrives on music and attracts performers from all over the world. These local men are playing Irish Traditional Music in Reilly's Pub. On the fiddle is Benny Monaghan and on the accordion is Edward McNamee (formerly of the Melody Aces Showband, Newtownstewart). Photo courtesy of Angus Mitchell.

Performing at the Emigrants' Wake Re-enactment are The McElhinneys, a popular group from Letterkenny.

Ulster–American Folk Park

The stage for the concert celebrating 25 years of the Park. The entertainers were The Nitty Gritty Dirt Band, the R. Cajun, the Zydeco Brothers and the Sharon Shannon Band.

The Omagh Community Youth Choir and a visiting American Choir from Milwaulkie perform in glorious sunshine on 20th July 2000 with Daryl Simpson conducting.

At the 25th Anniversary Celebrations this unique photograph, outside the Western Pennsylvania Log House, was taken of all the staff available to attend. Eric Montgomery (founder of the Park) is in the foreground (6th July, 2001).

Left Section: Front Row (l to r): Philip Mowat, Mr. John Winters, Mrs. Ursula Harron, Mr. Paul Harkin, Mrs. Roberta Maxwell, Mr. Noel Graham, Mr. Kevin Harpur, Mr. Ben Cobane
Top Row (l to r): Mr. Paul Billson, Mrs. Thelma Loane, Mrs. Angela Beattie, Mrs. Nancy Elkin, Mrs. Iris Fulton, Mrs. Hilary Mulholland, Mr. Mark Giles, Mrs. Ruby Todd, Mrs. Una Timoney.

Middle Section: Front Row (l to r): Mrs. Avril Cavanagh, Mrs. Ruby Hemphill, Mrs. Monica Winters.
Middle Row (l to r): Mrs. Marion Russell, Mrs. Mary Duncan, Mrs. Mary Forbes, Mrs. Margaret Magee, Mrs. Breege O'Sullivan.
Top Row (l to r): Mrs. Phyllis Jack, Miss Wendy McKelvey, Mrs. Maisie Patrick, Mrs. Patricia O'Donnell, Mrs. Marian McIvor.

Right Section: Front Row (l to r): Mr. John Bradley, Mrs. Rachel Craig, Mrs. Kathleen Ferguson, Mrs. Rita Wasson, Mr. Paddy Colgan, Miss Chris McIvor, Dr. Brian Lambkin, Mr. John Gilmour, Dr. Denis MacNeice.
Top Row (l to r): Mr. Jimmy Moore, Mr. Mickey Nugent, Mr. Clarence Fenton, Mrs. Betty Clarke, Mrs. Christine Johnston, Miss Belinda Mehaffey, Miss Fiona Casey, Miss Evelyn Cardwell, Mrs. Maggie Pinder.

178

Ulster–American Folk Park

St. Eugene's Brass and Reed Band from Omagh playing outside the main entrance to the Folk Park on the occasion of the Park's 30th Anniversary.

The Park has developed a programme of annual events.
The Christmas celebrations round the houses goes on for four days. This is the Omagh Music Society singing carols in the Presbyterian Meeting House with the Rev. John Murdoch conducting on 20th December, 2006.
(l to r): Julie Burton, Margaret Mitchell, Jean Murray, Eileen Brady, Father Kevin Mullan, Gwen Garrett, Roy Wilkinson, Michelle Davison.
Ref. "The Ulster–American Folk Park" by Jarrold Publishing, Norwich (1997)

CHAPTER 13

Charles Mullin (Solicitor, Omagh)
(the first person to be interred in Omagh Town Cemetery)
by John McCandless

The population of Omagh town was devastated on 3rd April, 1902 by the news of the death of Charles Mullin, aged 38, a local solicitor and son of the proprietor of the White Hart Hotel. Charles had lived all his life in Omagh. Being the son of the local hotel owner he was particularly well known, but he was also very popular. It is stated that he was a "centre for happiness and enjoyment", that he had "the power to hold people's attention and win their admiration and esteem" and that "his presence put life into social meetings whether private or public". The *Tyrone Constitution* reports that "not once in a century was a man given to a community with such a large nature, and so many popular gifts".

Charles Mullin's death was made ever more poignant by an event that occurred several weeks beforehand. Charles, in his civic capacity, had attended the consecration of the new cemetery at Dublin Road. On leaving the graveyard with his colleague, a D. A. Clements, Charles asked *"who do you think will be the first to enter through those gates?"* Little did anyone think that it would be Charles Mullin himself.

Shortly after the cemetery consecration Charles took ill. Initially it was not thought that the illness would develop into anything of a serious nature. He was confined to bed for a few days under the care of the local doctor. However, as his condition deteriorated and was diagnosed as "something akin to brain fever", an eminent doctor from Belfast was sent for, but all efforts to revive the sufferer were in vain and Charles Mullin died just two weeks after the onset of his illness.

The funeral that followed was the largest ever seen in Omagh. It is estimated that several thousand gathered at High Street and these were joined by hundreds more along the route. When the hearse entered the graveyard, the end of the procession was still at the Dublin Road laundry (close to the present Dublin Road corner).

Charles Mullin

At a later Service in First Omagh Presbyterian Church the words of Rev. A. Macafee reflect the immense impact that this death had on the Omagh community. He said in conclusion, "In a few days, in the very prime of his life, with so many friends, with so much love, and so much to make life happy, so much to live for and hope for, cut down suddenly by the stroke of death! It was unspeakably sad. It was hard for them to think that they would never see his well known form and genial face in their places of concourse again".

The official civic response to Charles Mullin's death arose from a proposal by fellow Urban Councillor Mr. D. A. Clements who proposed that his memory should be perpetuated by "raising a monument over his remains". A tombstone was duly commissioned and erected at Charles Mullin's grave. It stands at the top left end of the main driveway — *inscription reference page 184.*

The Inniskillings Memorial in High Street before removal to Drumragh Avenue. Charles Mullin helped to raise money for its erection in memory of those who died in the Boer War. Note closely the Mullin Fountain is just visible above the memorial on the left. It was removed in 1929.

Charles Mullin

In addition, although no appeal was ever officially launched, considerable sums of money were spontaneously donated against the sentiment that a monument to Mr. Mullin's memory should be erected in a public place. This resulted in the erection of an ornate drinking fountain in High Street close to the Courthouse and importantly opposite the White Hart Hotel *(see opposite)* where Charles Mullin had lived all of his short life.

This photograph (taken in 1923 in High Street) of a ceremony to remember the dead of the Great War. It shows clearly from the top the Mullin Drinking Fountain erected by the friends of Charles Mullin after his death in 1902 (it was removed in 1929). Below the fountain is a temporary memorial that ended up in the grounds of the British Legion in Campsie. The Boer War or Inniskillings Memorial stands lower down High Street and was erected in 1905. Charles Mullin is said to have raised funds for its erection.

Charles Mullin

Charles Mullin was admitted as a solicitor in 1887, having served his apprenticeship with H. H. Moore, later to be Clerk of the Crown and Peace for Cavan. It is known that Charles had an office in the White Hart Hotel (owned by his mother) in 1889 when he was aged 25. In the same year he had a professional address at 16 Bachelors Walk, Dublin. By 1894 he had moved to offices at 2 John Street and it is known that he progressively expanded his legal practice to Castlederg, Newtownstewart, Sixmilecross and Strabane.

Outside of his professional work Charles Mullin had many interests. These included Unionist politics, Free Masonry, the Orange Order, Y.M.C.A. and First Omagh Presbyterian Church. He also actively supported many local charities and he was an acknowledged authority on antiques and archaeology, on which he contributed regular articles in the *Tyrone Constitution* under the nom-de-plume "Max".

Charles was elected as a Town Commissioner in July 1895 and later as a member of Omagh Urban Council. He was the first County Councillor from Omagh under a new Act of Parliament at that time. He was a member of most of the local public Boards and Committees including the Asylum Committee and the Board of Management of Tyrone County Infirmary.

It is reported that one of his last public acts was to organise, with the assistance of several others, a tournament in aid of the monument to the Inniskilling Fusiliers that had been "an unqualified financial success".

The Mullin Drinking Fountain (circled) opposite the White Hart Hotel.

Charles Mullin

The White Hart Hotel

The White Hart Hotel in Omagh existed in 1824. At that time the owner was David Greer.

By 1856 the owner is listed as "Elizabeth Greer". The premises are described as a "Hotel and posting house" and the street is referred to as "Main Street".

By 1874 the proprietor was William Mullin. Mr. Mullin died between 1878 and 1882. The succeeding proprietor was Mrs. Mullin, his widow. Mrs. Mullin remained in this capacity until sometime between 1905 and 1909. The new owner after that time was Mr. Eli Barker.

William Mullin had a son, Charles and a daughter, Miss S. Mullin.

In Memory of
Charles Mullin
Solicitor, Omagh
who departed this life on the 3rd day of April, 1902, aged 38 years.
A Kind and Faithful Friend, Beloved of the poor and ever ready to promote the welfare of his native town.

This memorial has been erected by the friends who knew his generous and sterling character.

CHAPTER 14

The Mystery Train or The Sugar Train

by Rotarian Michael Pollard

The Mystery Train, sometimes known as "The Sugar Train" was a feature of Northern Ireland travel from the outbreak of the Second World War up to the mid-1950s.

The 1920s and 1930s had seen hard times in Northern Ireland with the setting up of the new State. Work was scarce and pay was low, with many families just managing to get by. There was no such thing as holidays for most people and even a day out was an annual event.

The coming of the Second World War changed all that. In late 1939 and in early 1940 Northern Ireland received a very large influx of service men and women from all three branches of the armed services. Most towns and villages were home to various battalions of the British Army, some 29 R.A.F. Air Bases were established in all counties in Northern Ireland and the Royal Navy used the ports as bases to fight "The Battle of the Atlantic".

The author with the late Tom McDevitte at the West Tyrone Historical Society in 1991.

The Mystery Train or The Sugar Train

This meant full employment for local people, in building camps, air bases and naval bases. When these establishments were up and running, thousands of Northern Ireland people obtained employment to service them and many thousands more were employed in factories all over the province, providing material for the forces. The shipbuilding and building of aircraft in Belfast boomed. All over the province factories made armaments and the clothing industry was at full stretch.

Work was hard but the difference was that it was plentiful with good wages and plenty of well-paid overtime. Soon people found themselves with some spare money and the weekends became a time for short breaks and days out.

The most popular day out was an excursion to the seaside. These were mostly by train as very few people had cars and no one had petrol except for essential work. The main excursions were to the holiday resorts all round the coast and many to the seaside resorts in Eire, such as Bundoran.

Food was scarce so the Great Northern Railway instituted a special excursion train known as "The Mystery Train". These excursions started from Belfast and ran to various towns across the border. The most popular destinations were Dundalk and Monaghan but trains also ran to Castleblaney, Clones, Cavan and Omeath in Co. Louth and Bundoran in Co. Donegal.

The Bundoran-Enniskillen line leaving Omagh (bottom of photograph) passing behind McGaghey Terrace. The line closed on 1st October, 1957 and the last train was pulled by 'Armagh No. 203'.

The Mystery Train or The Sugar Train

These excursions proved extremely popular and very well supported, so much so that as many as three or four ran from Belfast each weekend. As their popularity grew, so routes were set up from most stations in the North. The Great Northern Railway included excursions from Tyrone to Bundoran and Counties Cavan and Monaghan and on occasions, ran through the Sligo Leitrim line to Sligo. The Londonderry and Lough Swilly Railway ran weekend excursions from the city to Buncrana. The trains were huge and as many as three might run in one day.

The excursions served a number of purposes, the main one being a family day out and an opportunity to top up supplies of food, which were plentiful in Eire and scarce in Northern Ireland. Mother took her brood with her and brought back her and her children's full allowance of food. One of the main commodities brought back was sugar and each person was allowed 2 lb. hence the nickname "Sugar Train". Other items of food such as meat, jam, butter and many others were also brought back. In most of these there was a permissible allowance. When the Southern government was set up in 1922 it attempted to be as self-sufficient as possible, making the best use of agriculture. As well as dairy production it had a thriving sugarbeet industry, with four factories. This lasted until the last factory, in Mallow, closed in 2006. Sugar from sugarbeet was different from cane sugar in that it was much coarser and it was particularly good for jam making. Dairy products such as meat and butter, together with

IRVINESTOWN
U Class 4-4-0 No. 201 "Meath" passing with the Bundoran Express for Dublin.

The Mystery Train or The Sugar Train

ham and sugar, which were severely rationed in the North, were freshly available in the South.

Numerous stories are told of the skulduggery that went on in these trains where all sorts of items were smuggled back home, including items of clothing, which were rationed in Northern Ireland. The ladies sometimes wore enormous coats full of extra pockets and wide skirts, coming home much larger than when they left. Materials were hidden in parts of the train and even out of the windows. Some of the men dressed as priests since a priest or clergyman was seldom searched.

The Great Northern railway, who were making a handsome profit from these trains, played their part in calling them "Mystery Trains". They never advertised their destination so that the Customs were not forewarned to meet them, the result being that a large excursion train could arrive unexpectedly at a station where a Customs Post had only one or two officers on duty. There would be enough men on the train to see that the Custom official could do no more than a nominal search. The Great Northern Railway had several routes across the border so the train could make a circular route to again thwart the Customs officials. The railway staff had to know the movements of these trains but were sworn to secrecy and were happy to play their part as they were earning lucrative overtime.

KESH
PP Class 4-4-0 No. 50 pauses with a Bundoran to Enniskillen train in the early 1950s.

The Mystery Train or The Sugar Train

One aspect of these excursions to the South is less well known and is one of the reasons why the men joined the outings, as they would not have been as interested in smuggling food and clothes as the ladies were. Railway travel was well established in Ireland by the 1860s but long-distance travel was very slow. An example of this is the first through service from Dublin to Londonderry, established in March 1859, with a journey time of eight and a half hours. This meant frequent stops for refreshments and comfort stops. The trains ran at all hours and often outside licensing hours. A Licensing Act of 1872 stated "Nothing . . . shall preclude at any time at a railway station the sale of intoxicating liquors to persons arriving at or departing from stations by railroad".

This Act established the "bona fide traveller" who was defined by the Act as "a passenger at a railway station more than five miles from where he or she had lodged the previous night". The net result was that travellers could eat and drink at all hours, seven days a week, provided they were at specially licensed premises and were more than five miles from home or their last night lodgings and had a valid rail ticket.

Many of the larger railway stations had their own hotels or restaurants but where they did not, a local hotel or public house adjacent to the station could apply for this licence. Nearly every town with a railway station had a "Railway Hotel" or a "Railway Bar" for use by the bona fide traveller. These premises were, of

PETTIGO
PP Class 4-4-0 No. 73 has just arrived with the 11.00 from Enniskillen and the fireman is on the platform watching the driver recouple his engine to the train before moving off to the sidings. Intending pilgrims to Lough Derg are on the platform. The date was 27th July, 1959. Photo by Drew Donaldson.

The Mystery Train or The Sugar Train

course, obliged to open at all hours for the convenience of bona fide travellers and it was not uncommon for the police to visit the premises to check that anyone drinking outside normal hours had a valid rail ticket. This could be flouted as the Act allowed the traveller to drink before or after a journey, so someone really thirsty could get a ticket from a railway station to the nearest station more than five miles away and benefit from the Act. Many of these hotels and bars still use the name "Railway" the best local example being The Railway Hotel in Enniskillen, which is situated opposite the site of the old station.

This Act was not included in the Northern Ireland statutes when the State was set up but continued in the South and was revised in 1962 to encourage rail travel for outings at weekends. There is no mention of the Act since then so it probably still exists. The only special licence in Northern Ireland, apart from N.I. Railways' restaurant cars, is granted to The Railway Preservation Society of Ireland who run a restaurant car and bar in their vintage excursion train.

In Omagh, the "excursion train" ran at weekends, long after food rationing ended and right up to the closing of the Enniskillen line and the cross-border lines in 1957. The trains ran to Bundoran Junction and then either to Clones, Cavan or Monaghan or left the main line at the junction and ran to Bundoran. In later days the excursions were on Sundays to Bundoran and were mainly a day out for those who wished to benefit from the "bona fide" regulations.

A GNR advertising poster of a railcar at Leggs, Co. Fermanagh with Lough Erne in the background. This was the nearest the railway came to the lough en route to Castlecaldwell and Belleek where it crossed the River Erne.

The Mystery Train or The Sugar Train

CASTLECALDWELL
P Class 4-4-0 is unusually in the Up Loop here while working the 10.30 a.m. from Bundoran to Enniskillen on 1st August, 1955.

BELLEEK
U Class 4-4-0 No. 203 "Armagh" restarts the 8.45 a.m. from Enniskillen to Bundoran on 22nd June, 1957. Percy Wray is on the platform.

The Mystery Train or The Sugar Train

BALLYSHANNON
PP Class 4-4-0 No. 74 waits with the 2.10 p.m. from Enniskillen to Bundoran on 2nd August, 1956.

Members of Culmore and O'Kane Park Residents' Association launch an entrance feature to remember the last train to Bundoran 50 years ago in 1957.
Standing (l to r): Sean Begley (Chairman of O.D.C.), Rosella Kelly, Kieran Gallagher, Kathleen Colton, Carmel Sharkey, Frank Gillease (Chairman).
Kneeling (l to r): Melyn Waddell (Ground Work Northern Ireland), Mark McGrath, Jimmy O'Kane, Danny McSorley (Chief Executive, O.D.C.).
Bundoran Ref. "Images of Omagh" Vol. 13, Page 88 — Photographs Copyright: Charles Friel Collection.

The Mystery Train or The Sugar Train

The train travelled through Bundoran Junction to Irvinestown and Kesh, where it crossed the border near Pettigo, and back into Fermanagh to Castlecaldwell and Belleek, crossing the border again to Ballyshannon and finally to Bundoran. The Northern Ireland Customs were at Kesh and the Southern at Ballyshannon. Customs Officers were stationed at Pettigo, Castlecaldwell and Belleek but they only searched travellers who boarded or alighted from trains at these stations.

SOUTH OF THE BORDER DOWN PETTIGO WAY
by Frank McCrory

South of the Border down Pettigo way
That's where the folks get all the Free State sugar to put in their tay,
They've plenty of sugar, at least so they say
South of the Border down Pettigo way.

When at the Border our excursion train stopped
Into our third class carriage the Customs man then smartly hopped,
He cried, "Have you anything you should declare?"
"For if you're smuggling you'd better beware".

Then I lied when I answered "nothing"
As I cautiously rose to my feet,
But he sighed as he answered "Baloney",
"You've half a stone under that seat".

He had me cornered and what could I say?
He looked at me quite cross, and then he slowly turned away,
"Do you come from Omagh?, Quick, tell me I pray"
The Customs man whispered down Pettigo way.

When I said, "Yes I do come from Omagh"
Then he grasped me tight by the arm,
"I was born there myself — there's your sugar,
"I'll do an Omagh man no harm".

There'll be a famine, the old folk all say,
There's no butter, sugar, bread, tobacco, coffee or tay,
When they ration the porter, all together we'll stray
South of the Border down Pettigo way.

(see page 237)

CHAPTER 15

Omagh Health Centre
The First Generation

When World War II ended in 1945 the GP services were still run under the dispensary system. Dr. Bernard Lagan was in charge in Omagh, Dr. Fred Mitchell in Beragh and Dr. James Cunningham in Carrickmore.

All medical services were paid for except those with Medical Cards.

Medical drugs, especially liquid medicines, were often made up by the doctors in their own surgeries which were usually in their own homes. Only a few had the luxury of a nurse.

In hospital, if you required an operation you had to paid for it and also for the bed you occupied. If you couldn't pay the total amount then instalments were allowed depending on your means.

The Labour Government came to power after the war and one of the most important Acts they were to introduce was the National Health Service Act that created a free health service for everyone.

The Health Centre before the removal of the trees.

Omagh Health Centre — The First Generation

It didn't change things for General Practitioners immediately except for the free element of the service. The GP still continued after 1948 to operate from his own surgery usually in his own home, but some GPs came together to form partnerships that would allow for more organisation of their working day which previously was a 7 days a week, 24 hours a day. Many doctors didn't have surgery hours and were present in their surgery in the morning, afternoon and evening for as long as it took to see the patients that came. Home visits were done between these hours.

Telephones were uncommon and when home visits were required, someone was sent to the doctor's home to leave the request and the particulars of the problem.

In Omagh in the 1950s and 1960s the GPs met infrequently to discuss running their practices but there was no general rota just the practices that had more than two partners working together.

The government was always working to improve the conditions of both doctor and patient and in the 1960s the idea of the Health Centre was suggested and several were built in different areas of the U.K. on a trial basis.

The mid 60s saw the first of the Health Centres or Group Practices appear in Strabane followed by Ballymoney. In Omagh the County Medical Officer, Dr. Balmer had a brother open the first Health Centre in Belfast at Finaghy with four other local GPs. He discussed the situation with Dr. Charles Tully who went to

Dr. Roy McClements presenting Hilary Price with a gift on the occasion of her engagement in September 1977.

Omagh Health Centre — The First Generation

have a look at the Finaghy premises and was more than impressed.

The local GPs got together and showed their interest in building their own Health Centre. A meeting with Dr. Fergus McKeown, Chief County Medical Officer and Bertie Parke the County Secretary was held and a decision made to look for a suitable site and ask for an architect to design a building suitable for the needs of the doctors and the local medical services.

The site was acquired on the Mountjoy Road and the architects were Ostick & Williams who were, at that time, the County Architects who had designed the County Hall. The building was started in 1969 and built by McCann Brothers, a local firm, for £150,000.

It was opened in April 1971 by the then Stormont Minister of Health, Mr. Fitzsimmons.

Omagh's Health Centre was the fifth to be opened in Northern Ireland and was the largest at that time and the first to have a pharmacy on the premises.

The present building has undergone extensive renovations in recent years to keep up with the needs of the town's growing population.

Over the years many staff have come and gone for one reason and another. The following pages are a reminder of some of the doctors and staff who served the population of Omagh during the first generation of the present Health Centre.

The first person you meet when you enter the Health Centre is the telephonist — but do you know her name? This is Carol Smyth who has been in the post for 20 years. The first telephonist was the late Frances Devlin who came to the Health Centre from the Tyrone County Hospital.

Omagh Health Centre — The First Generation

Dr. Charles Tully's Retirement Presentation in 1977.

Back Row (l to r): Dr. Mark Fraser, Dr. Aidan Lagan, Dr. Bill McMullan, Dr. Brendan Kelly, Dr. Haldane Mitchell.
Front Row (l to r): Dr. Maura McMullan, Dr. James Fulton, Dr. Charles Knox Tully, Dr. Josephine Allen, Dr. Pat O'Neill.

Dr. Charles Tully's Retirement Presentation in 1977.

Back Row (l to r): Mary Quinn, Molly Armstrong, Gertie Shortt, Sheena Kearney, Marie Grugan, May Vance.
Front Row (l to r): Una Deveney, Carmel McGrath, Dr. Tully, Hilary Price, Eileen McElroy.

Omagh Health Centre — The First Generation

Dr. F. H. McMullan speaking at his own Retirement Presentation on 4th February, 1987.

Dr. Jean Hendly retires in June 1988.
Dr. Aidan Lagan is Master of Ceremonies.

Omagh Health Centre — The First Generation

Dorothy Bradley (née Martin) receives a presentation from Dr. Haldane Mitchell on the occasion of her leaving Omagh to live in Carrickfergus in 1990.
Also in photo are Kyra Chesney, Carmel McGrath and Julie Irvine.

The ever popular Mary McCullough (née McGinn) retires on 31st March, 2000.
Also in photo are Dorothy Bradley, Drew Hawkes, Larry Mongan and Tommy Farmer.

WEEKENDS ON CALL

It's a strange fact, but true, that when Saturdays come
Folks who've been ill all the week just succumb
To temptation to pick up their phone and relate
To the poor Duty Doctor "I'm ill – It won't wait".

"How long have you had it?", I patiently ask,
"Since Sunday or Monday – I didn't think it would last!"
"You've seen your own Doctor? What did he have to say?"
"Well, he's always so busy I just stayed away!"

It's rare for a "weekend-on-call" to go past
Without some visiting relative ringing to ask,
"Can you visit my Mother, Aunt, Great Uncle Will?
He's not fit to live by himself – he's too ill!".

It's never your patient and when you get there
You find he needs physio or maybe sheltered care,
You explain that on Sunday there just isn't any way
To contact Social Services – it must be a weekday.

The aim of these few verses is for patients just to say
WEEKENDS ARE FOR EMERGENCIES which occur on that day,
If these facts could be remembered then weekends won't be so bad
And we'll get there even quicker to treat your real sick DAD!

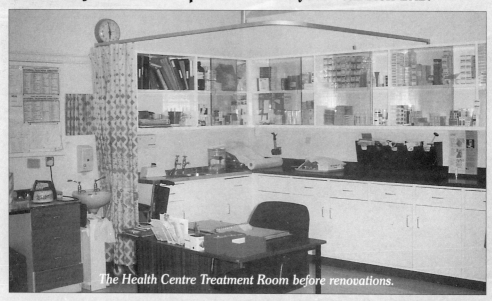

The Health Centre Treatment Room before renovations.

Omagh Health Centre — The First Generation

Dr. James K. Fulton's Retirement Presentation in 1984.
(l to r): Sheena Kearney, Gertie Shortt, Dr. Oliver Hinds, Mrs. Mary Fulton, Dr. James K. Fulton, Carmel McGrath.

Helen Breslin retires as Senior Receptionist in Dr. McMullan's practice on 14th February, 1997.
(l to r): Doctors Bill and Maura McMullan, Helen Breslin, Dr. Pat O'Neill and Dr. Bill McCallion.

Dr. Aidan Lagan's Retirement Presentation in November 1991.

Standing (l to r): Una McSwiggan, Dr. Oliver Hinds, Nurse Margaret McCartan, Nurse Bernie McQuaid, Dr. Nigel Pollock, Geraldine Colton, Nurse Lily O'Boyle, Dr. Tom Connolly, Frances Arnold, Janet O'Neill, Marie Slane.

Seated (l to r): Dr. Kay Lagan and Dr. Aidan Lagan.

Omagh Health Centre — The First Generation

Dr. Lagan's Retirement Party in the Royal Arms Hotel on 14th March, 1992,

Dr. Brendan Kelly speaking on behalf of Dr. Lagan's colleagues.

Declan O'Kane of the Knotty Pine String Band on violin.

Dr. Wesley Nabney (Newtownstewart) speaking on behalf of his country colleagues.

Dr. Haldane Mitchell Retires in 1996

Dr. Mitchell you're leaving us too
We meet to say farewell to you
To work with you it was a pleasure
Our respect you've earned in greatest measure.

With gentle touch you attended the weak
The old, the ill, the poor, the meek
Each patient you treated with utmost respect
No one to you was a 'social reject'.

Every morning at a half past eight
You were never ever late
No one ever saw you cross
You will be Omagh General's loss.

With video camera you were ace
Recording all around the place
Each year the Doctor did record
A tape of the General and beyond.

You captured the joy and sheer delights
Of Omagh Town with Christmas lights
Shop windows decked with festive fare
For those who couldn't travel there.

You extended your role on Christmas Day
Our favourite Santa Claus to play
You also brought along your wife
To sing Carols with all her might.

We know you do not want a fuss
For the time and effort spent with us
On behalf of the patients may we say
Thank you Doctor, you made their day.

The staff also your praise do sing
When the telephone we did often ring
Your attention and devotional care
Was appreciated by all there.

We have read the articles you did write
Of bygone days, some none too bright
Your retirement therefore holds no mystery
As you pursue the local history.

May health and happiness be a bliss
We at the General Dr. Mitchell will miss
So now let us whilst we can
Bid farewell to nature's Gentleman.

Composed and presented by Nurse Jean Thompson, Staff Omagh General Hospital
April 1996

Omagh Health Centre — The First Generation

*Receptionist Mary Horisk leaves to take up a post in the Tyrone County Hospital
(25th April, 1997).*
Back Row (l to r): Carmel McGrath, Sharon McGurk, Ursula Davidson, Fiona McAleer, Marie McNulty.
Front Row (l to r): Louise McAleer, Mary Horisk, Aileen Conway, Helen Lowe, Leisl O'Reilly.

*Tommy Farmer (seen here with his wife Maura) retires on 19th November, 1997
after 25 years as administrator of the Health Centre*

Omagh Health Centre — The First Generation

Dr. Pat O'Neill's Retirement Party in the Royal Arms Hotel on 13th November, 1998.
Back Row (l to r): Dr. Bill McCallion, Tommy Farmer, Eamon McCann, Dr. Patrick Quinn, Dr. Michael
Kemp, Michael Deehan, Dr. Eamon McMullan, Dr. Brendan McDonald.
Front Row (l to r): Dr. Tom Connolly, Dermot McCann (Pharmacist), Dr. Desmond Gormley, Richard
Andrew, Dr. Oliver Hinds, Dr. Pat O'Neill, Dr. Paul Bradley, Dr. Pat Loughrey (Drumquin).

Back Row (l to r): Margaret Mitchell, Dr. Jo Deehan, Dr. Maureen Halliday, Dr. Paula Gallagher, Jill
Connolly, Agnes O'Neill, Dr. Alison Noone, Helen Breslin, Tina McCrory, Ruth Kemp.
Front Row (l to r): Mrs. I. Hassan, Ethna Loughrey, Mary Hinds, Maura Farmer, Patricia McCallion.

Omagh Health Centre — The First Generation

Section of practice refurbishment being officially opened by Richard Scott (Chairman of the Sperrin Lakeland Trust) on 25th October, 1999.
Back Row (l to r): Ann Breen, Ursula Davidson, Rosemary Rogers, Fiona McAleer.
Front Row (l to r): Carmel McGrath, Leisl O'Reilly, Noreen Oliver (Nurse), Aileen Conway, Sharon McGurk.

Modelling new uniforms.
(l to r); Julie Irvine, Ann McAleer, Liesl O'Reilly, Catriona McPhillips, Carmel McGrath, Aileen Conway.

Staff, past and present, taken at the rear of the Health Centre in 1995.

Standing (l to r):   Dr. I. Hassan, Dr. Tom Connolly, Dr. Desmond Gormley, Dr. Brendan McDonald, Dr. Eamon McMullan, Dr. Bill McCallion, Dr. Michael kemp, Dr. Nigel Pollock, Dr. Paul Bradley, Dr. Michael McCavert, Dr. Pat O'Neill, Tommy Farmer (Unit Administrator).

Seated (l to r):   Dr. Fergus McKeown (County Medical Officer, retired), Dr. Aidan Lagan, Dr. Haldane Mitchell, Dr. Maura McMullan, Joyce McAskie (previous Administrator), Dr. Bill McMullan, Dr. Brendan Kelly.

DOCTOR JAMES KERR FULTON

BORN 21st OCTOBER 1924 DIED 13TH MARCH 1992

In Loving Memory Of
A DEAR WIFE AND MOTHER
DR. KAY LAGAN
(NÉE SORENSEN)
DIED 15TH DECEMBER 1998
AGED 71 YEARS
A DEAR HUSBAND AND FATHER
DR. AIDAN LAGAN
DIED 27TH FEBRUARY 2002
AGED 79 YEARS

They Rest from Their Labours

TULLY
In Loving Memory Of
CHARLES ALEXANDER KNOX TULLY, M.B.,B.CH.,M.R.C.G.P.
DIED 7TH AUGUST 1980. AGED 57 YEARS.

McMULLAN
IN LOVING MEMORY OF
DR. F. H. McMULLAN (BILL) DIED 12TH MARCH 1999
DR. M. B. McMULLAN (MAURA) DIED 30TH SEPTEMBER 1999
THEIR INFANT DAUGHTER ANTOINETTE DIED 15TH JUNE 1964

209

CHAPTER 16

Andersons of the Cross

The town grew up round Bawntown Castle which was the residence of Lord Audley, who was (in 1601) created Earl of Castlehaven. The Manor of Ffinney or Koragh now Sixmilecross was surveyed in 1596–9 and patented to Lord Audley and his wife Elizabeth in 1601, under Queen Elizabeth. Ancestors of the Earl of Belmore purchased the Manor of Sixmilecross in 1656, but the castle grounds passed to Beresford, afterwards to the Gorge family by marriage, while in recent years it formed part of the Verner Estate. The hill of Tullyneil immediately adjoining the Presbyterian Church, is said to be the centre of Ulster.

Dunmoyle Castle was at one time the summer residence of the Right Hon. Mr. Justice Ross. Erected by his father-in-law Col. Deane Mann, J.P. in 1854 it is situated three miles from Sixmilecross.

It is thought that the Andersons came to Northern Ireland through a Joseph Anderson of Paisley, Scotland. He flourished as a merchant and his son Archibald enlisted as one of the Scottish yeomen under Sir Paul Gore for service in Northern Ireland to which he came in 1602.

After this with others, remained and more than 10 generations of his present day descendants.

Ref.: "Anderson of Flush & Bawn",
Sixmilecross, Co. Tyrone 1543–1977
by Robert Hall Anderson 1900.

Revised Edition by J. G. T. Anderson 1977
Printed by Tyrone Constitution, Omagh

King Anderson, brother of George (Omagh)
at his home in Tandragee, Sixmilecross.

Aerial photo of Sixmilecross.

Andersons of the Cross

The haggard, Tandragee, Sixmilecross in April 1934. (l to r): King Anderson and daughter Lily. In front of the henhouse are Mary Anne Anderson (wife of King) and sister of the late Mrs. Pollock, Omagh; Joe Anderson, Cecil Anderson and George Anderson.

Sixmilecross Fair in September 1934 — George was buying horses for his Omagh business, the dealing was done by a Fintona Horse Dealer and agreed by George. (l to r); Joe Anderson (cousin), Fintona Horse Dealer, Charles Anderson, Cecil Anderson, King Anderson, George Anderson.

Family Group at Anderson Wedding on Wednesday, 24th August, 1935.

Standing (l to r): Bennett (photographer), Pomeroy, John Henry Anderson (brother of Rose Pollock), Joe Anderson (member of O.D.C.), Freda Anderson, Isobel Anderson, Lily Anderson (sister of Cecil the groom and postmistress in Sixmilecross for years), Mrs. G. Anderson, — Watson (lived on the Derry Road), Fanny Ellison (Pomeroy, father and rate collector), Mrs. John Henry Anderson (a Hutchinson from Rosnamuck. ——, Mrs. C. A. Anderson, Mrs. McLaughlin (sister of Mrs. Pollock (mother of 'Bare Legged Joe' of W. F. Marshall fame), Peg Johnston, Charles Anderson.

Sitting (l to r): Mr. McMullan (father of the bride), Duncan Anderson (brother of the groom), Groom, Bride: Dorothy Ellison, Mrs. McMullan (mother of the bride).

213

Andersons of the Cross

Wedding of James Cecil Anderson and Ella McMullan at Carrickmore Parish Church on Wednesday, 24th August, 1935. Photograph at Corvey Lodge. Wedding conducted by Rev. N. St. G. Sides, C.M., M.A., assisted by Rev. J. Cockrill, M.A., Sixmilecross. Eldest son of King Anderson, Tandragee, Sixmilecross; Frances M. E. (Ella) only child of Mr. and Mrs. Robert McMullan, Nine Mile House, Tirooney, Carrickmore.

George Anderson, Sam Deery and William McFarland at Sixmilecross Fair in 1935.

Andersons of the Cross

Ella, Cecil and Baby Ivan (7¹/₂ months old) at Tirooney in 1939.
Ivan would live to become headmaster in Sixmilecross Primary School, only to die in the recent troubles near his home on 21st May, 1987 (aged 47).
He is buried in St. Michael's Parish Church graveyard, Sixmilecross.

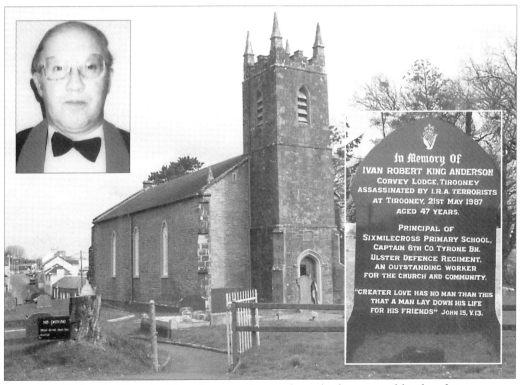

In Memory Of
IVAN ROBERT KING ANDERSON
CORVEY LODGE, TIROONEY
ASSASSINATED BY I.R.A. TERRORISTS
AT TIROONEY, 21ST MAY 1987
AGED 47 YEARS.

PRINCIPAL OF
SIXMILECROSS PRIMARY SCHOOL.
CAPTAIN 6TH CO. TYRONE BN.
ULSTER DEFENCE REGIMENT.
AN OUTSTANDING WORKER
FOR THE CHURCH AND COMMUNITY.

"GREATER LOVE HAS NO MAN THAN THIS
THAT A MAN LAY DOWN HIS LIFE
FOR HIS FRIENDS" JOHN 15, V.13.

St. Michael's Church, Sixmilecross. Insets: Ivan Anderson and his headstone.

CENTENARY ADDRESSES
DELIVERED BY
REV. W. F. MARSHALL, B.A., LL.B., M.R.I.A.
of Castlerock on 20th October, 1946
TO MARK THE
100th ANNIVERSARY
OF THE BUILDING OF
SIXMILECROSS PRESBYTERIAN CHURCH

MORNING ADDRESS

When my young friend, the minister here, gave me a generous invitation to conduct the services on this day, he indicated that I might be able to say something about the history of the congregation and Mr. Marshall.

I'll begin with a word or two about the Parish of Termonmaguirke. You know, of course, that Termon was land set apart for the upkeep of a church and that the termon for this parish consisted of certain townlands in the neighbourhood of Carrickmore which were tenanted by the family of McGurk. And since the termon was near Carrickmore, it gave the name to that district. Now Termon was formerly, and quite properly, pronounced Tarmon, so that it was easily corrupted by the people into Carmon, and now all of us who were bred in these parts find it far easier to talk about Carmon than about Carrickmore. It's also interesting to note that the first Christian Church in the parish was probably founded in Carmon by that great Ulsterman, St. Columbkille, and if not by him, then certainly by one of his disciples.

Ireland was divided into parishes 800 years ago, so ours is a very old parish. Seven hundred years ago it paid to the Pope an annual tax of 2/8 which, of course, would represent a very much larger sum in our money. Before the Plantation there were two churches within the parish bounds, one in Carrickmore, which was the Parish Church, and one in Clogherney, which seems to have been a chapel of ease.

A Very Big Parish

It's not only an old parish, it's a very big parish. Before the present parish of Clogherney was carved out, it comprised over 70 townlands. It stretched from Innishatieve to Ranelly, from Loughmacrory to Seskinore, from Aghnagar and Curr to Drumnakilly. It contained the present Church of Ireland parish of Termon at Carrickmore, the parishes of Sixmilecross and Drumnakilly and the parish of Clogherney, with its attendant Church at Seskinore. I should have said the greater part of the parish of Sixmilecross. Now, 300 years ago, or slightly less, the population of this big parish was very small, not much more than 200 families. And, prior to the Siege of Derry, I can only discover 32 Protestant families resident in the parish. The number is probably even less than that, for some of the names are registered in the Hearth Rolls and Subsidy Rolls as labourers or servants. It's clear, then, that prior to the Siege of Derry the whole parish population was small, and the Protestant population was tiny.

Andersons of the Cross

Most of these Protestant families, or so-called families, were in the lower end of the parish. Only seven of them lived in our congregational area here, and it's not surprising to find that four of the seven were Andersons, one in Kilcam, one in Cooley, one in Sixmilecross and one in Aghnaglea. There may have been only three Anderson families, for the John Anderson and his wife who are returned for Kilcam may be the same people as the John Anderson and his wife who are returned for Sixmilecross. But this is not certain. There was another Anderson family down at Tullyrush, which makes at least four families in the parish, and there may have been two cousins who had the same Christian name. The other families were named Holmes, Wood and Drummond. In the lower end of the parish there were Watsons, Givans, Perrys, Clarkes, Dunlaps and several others, and there were no Protestants at all farther up the parish than Aghnaglea.

You can see now what the position was less than 300 years ago — about 30 Protestant families in this huge parish of over 70 townlands — and you will not find it hard to believe what I said recently in another place, that in a few years after the Battle of the Boyne at least 50,000 people flocked over from Scotland into Ulster to fill up parishes like ours that had previously only a small population either of Irish, English or Scots.

Now, of these 30 families, the Presbyterian Church must have had its share, because there was a Presbyterian minister in the parish as early as 33 years before the Siege of Derry. His name was the Rev. Robert Wilson, and he was ordained in 1655 to minister to the Presbyterians in Termon and in Omagh. This man died in Derry during the Siege. He was only five years in Termon and Omagh, for he was called to Strabane in 1660, and for some years the Presbyterians here had to share a minister with various other congregations, until in due time they got a minister of their own. Where they worshipped during the early period is not known, but there was a stone in the old Dervaghroy Meetinghouse which has the date 1720. It is surmised that this stone was brought from a still older church which (tradition says) stood in a field in Laragh, called Meetinghouse Field.

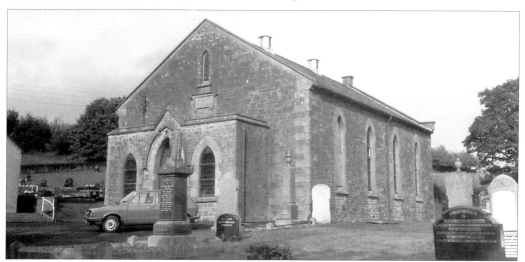

Sixmilecross Presbyterian Church.

Andersons of the Cross

You understand then, that the earliest Presbyterian congregation in the parish was the congregation now known as Clogherney, formerly called Dervaghroy and originally called Termon or Carmon. And it was natural that the first church should be centred there, for in those early days it was in that lower end of the parish that the most of the Presbyterians were to be found.

I trust you have not found this long preamble wearisome. It was necessary to burden you with it for I wanted to make it plain to you that there was a time when the Sixmilecross Presbyterians worshipped with the congregation now known as Clogherney, the historic name for which is Termon.

Well, at last, I can speak about Sixmilecross. But even here I find that I must begin with another preamble. Over 300 years ago the first Presbytery of our Church met at Carrickfergus. Quite soon other Presbyteries were formed, and these, joined together, made a Synod. It was called the Synod of Ulster. There was no General Assembly till 106 years ago and for a long time the Synod of Ulster was the Supreme Court of our Church.

But over in Scotland, a lot of Presbyterians began to think that the preaching in the Church of Scotland was not warm enough or evangelical enough, so they left it and formed another which was popularly known as the Secession Church. This movement spread to Ireland over a couple of hundred years ago, and Secession churches were founded all over Ulster. These churches were formed into Presbyteries and the Presbyteries were united in a Synod, called the Secession Synod.

Interior of the church.
Note the oil lamps on either side of the pulpit used in the days before electricity.

Andersons of the Cross

Here then in Ireland we had two large Presbyterian Churches, one represented by the Synod of Ulster, and the other by the Secession Synod. They were quite separate, and between them there was great rivalry and often sharp competition. This lasted till 106 years ago, when the two Synods were united and the united body was named the General Assembly of the Presbyterian Church in Ireland.

This church in Sixmilecross was a Secession Church. The church in Clogherney belonged to the other Synod, the Synod of Ulster.

Nearly 200 Years Old

When may we be said to have begun here? It's not possible to give an exact date, but we are on safe ground when we say that we are very nearly 200 years old. Over in Scotland, in Stirling, there was a meeting of Presbytery 197 years ago, which indirectly made changes in the Presbyterian history of Sixmilecross. At that meeting the Rev. Thomas Clarke was ordained by the Secession Presbytery of Glasgow as a Home Missionary in Ireland. He was the minister soon of a Secession Church in Co. Monaghan but he travelled all over that county and County Armagh and County Tyrone, preaching at meetings which eventually developed into Secession congregations. It was he who formed our church here.

He was a little Scotsman who rode a shaggy pony and wore a Highland bonnet, and the late James McLean, whose stock of local tradition was prodigious, used to tell me stories he had heard from his grandfather about "Bonnety" Clarke, and how often he was seen galloping over the Tyrone roads. After 15 years' service in Ireland, he emigrated to America and took with him a large part of his congregation.

I have in my possession a pamphlet written by Dr. Clarke. It is Secession propaganda and is dated 1751. But the really interesting thing about it is that it states on the title page that it can be purchased from Mr. John Anderson in Sixmilecross. Now that is direct evidence that 195 years ago, there was the nucleus of a Secession congregation in Sixmilecross. Twelve years later they called a minister, in 1762, but they were not able to afford a minister of their own. Sixmilecross and Clogher formed a united charge and Clogher included Ballymagrane, which is on the Caledon side of Aughnacloy. It's interesting to note that our historic name is also Termon, for it is so that we are described in the Secession records, but we soon preferred geography to antiquity, and called ourselves Sixmilecross.

We called a minister, as I have said, in 1762. He was the Rev. Joseph Kerr, but he probably didn't care for galloping from here to Ballymagrane and from that to Clogher, for he settled in Ballygoney. We tried again in 1764, and called the Rev. James McAuley, but he went to Castleblayney. We tried again in 1766, and called the Rev. John Rogers, but he went to Dr. Clarke's old congregation in Co. Monaghan.

Period Of Confusion

A period of confusion seems to have ensued for the next ten years, during which apparently Sixmilecross was united with Aughentaine and in May 1776, the Rev. Thomas Dickson was installed here as minister of the united charge. The Rev. Felix Quinn preached the sermon, and the Rev. John Rogers conducted the service.

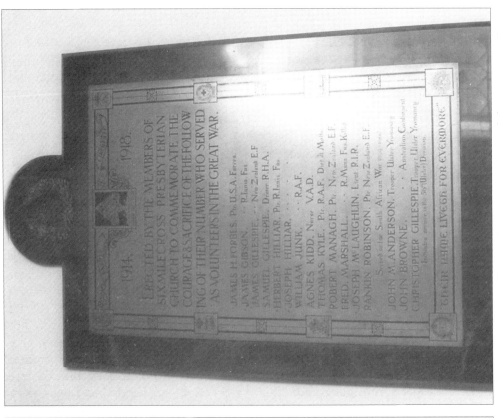

World War I Commemorative Plaques to those who served and gave the supreme sacrifice and were members of the congregation.

Andersons of the Cross

Sixmilecross promised to pay Mr. Dickson £23 1s 6d of stipend and Aughentaine was to pay him £18 2s 6d, together with eighteen and a half barrels of oats, Mr. Dickson's salary was therefore meagre by present day standards but that's not the way to judge it. We must judge it with relation to the fall in value of money, to our increased opportunities for spending it and to the universal rise in the quality of our living. On this view of it, I have no doubt that Mr. Dickson was far better off than his successor today. He stayed here about seven years after which he was called to Sandholes. I have often thought it likely that the Dickson family at the Slate Quarry may have been his descendants.

But now that I have shown you a congregation in being, with a minister, I must pause to ask a question: "Where did this congregation worship?"

Meetings At Beragh

Lord Belmore declared that the first meetings were held in the house of Mr. Peebles of Beragh corn mill. The late James Forbes, of Ballintrain, whose memory would have taken him back till long before the Battle of Waterloo, told my father that the meetings were first held at Beragh at the house of a man who had a corn mill. Dr. Latimer, who probed deeply into church histories, states that the meetings were first held in the house of a Mr. Peebles in the townland of Beragh, near what was known as the Well Lane. The truth is bound to be somewhere among these three stories. Two of them mention a Mr. Peebles and two of them mention a corn mill. Perhaps the Beragh people can solve the puzzle about the mill, but there is no need to suppose that Mr. Peebles' house must have been alongside his mill. The house may have been near the Well Lane, and the mill quite a distance away. It may be said, too, that there was no Well Lane in the middle of the 18th century, because there was no Beragh.

Dr. Latimer tells us that following these meetings at Beragh, there were meetings held in the Market-house at Sixmilecross. Now the present Market-house was built in 1854, so it is ruled out. We're dealing with a period that is a hundred years before that. Where was the Market-house then? Mr. Willie Anderson was able to tell me that the former Market-house was in the late Mr. Joseph Anderson's yard, and used to belong to Joseph Anderson's maternal grandfather. But he was also able to tell me that there was an even older one still, and that it stood somewhere in the Horse Fair, on the premises of Mr. Armstrong. We may take it, I think, that it was in this oldest Market-house that the meetings were held.

They seem to have worshipped in these unsuitable places for at least 30 years, for it was not till 1786 that they built a church. It was a thatched house with a clay floor, and it had turf sods for seats.

That was just after Mr. Dickson had left them and had gone to Sandholes. Dr. Latimer says that Mr. Dickson's manse was a mud house at Cess Hill on the Beragh road, and not far from the old fort. We mustn't be too sorry for Mr. Dickson. A mud cottage, well plastered and well thatched, and properly looked after was nothing to look down on. It was cool in summer and warm in winter, and it was probably as good as any, and better than most in the district at that time for we had no gentry in our district and no resident rector or curate. I hasten to add that the Protestant unity which made my ministry here so pleasant, is of no mushroom growth, for on the 5th of June, 1786, the Parish Vestry voted £10 towards the building of the new Presbyterian Church. Over 40 years later, we had the pleasure of returning that compliment in a fashion that will be described when my story reaches that far.

But it has already reached as far as is bearable to you this morning. We have passed the ministry of Mr. Dickson, and are approaching that of the Rev. Lewis Brown, about whom many old tales lingered till modern time. I hope to take up the story from that point this evening.

THE EVENING ADDRESS

This evening I have to complete the story which I began this morning. Where did we leave off? It was at the departure of Rev. Thomas Dickson in 1784, and the building of the new church in 1786. It will seem very strange to you to hear that after Mr. Dickson left, there was a vacancy for eight years, but it will sound even stranger that it was during this vacancy that the congregation tackled the formidable task of building a church. I don't think a task of that kind would be attempted anywhere now without the leadership of a minister. Maybe in those days congregations needed less of a spur and were more ready to do things by themselves. Maybe they had just a little more money than usual, for the long war with America, France, Spain and Holland had ended the year before Mr. Dickson left, and farm produce had fetched war prices. But I think there was a more obvious reason than either of these. A congregation could save money in a vacancy. Sunday supplies come cheaper than a minister who had to be paid stipend. Much of the stipend could be saved and in 1786 and the four years that followed, even a little stipend would go a long way towards building a church. For if the people were not well-to-do, and they certainly had very few of that class — still labour was cheap, and materials were cheap, and the house itself was cheap. If they had a roof over their heads and walls to keep out the wind — these were the main things, and they looked for little more. A carpenter could make a simple pulpit and the people could sit on turf sods. Let us not sneer so much at some of our unlovely church buildings. We had to pay for them, and they were all that we could afford.

Near the end of 1792, the Rev. Lewis Brown was installed here by the Upper Tyrone Presbytery. He had been ordained in Dublin four years before and had ministered acceptably to a congregation in that city. It was a big change for him, but he fulfilled his ministry here for 44 years. No minister, except Mr. Junk (see plaque opposite), has served here for as much as half that period. He retired in 1836, and died 15 years later at the advanced age of 91.

Mr. Brown lived here in stirring times. For the first 23 years of his ministry there was almost continual war. War against revolutionary France, the long struggle against Napoleon, the great rebellion in Ireland in 1789, the great famine of 1823, and then, at the close of his long life, the dreadful famine of 1846–47. I wish we had him here for a few hours to tell us what Sixmilecross was like, and what its social history was in those eventful years. We are utterly destitute of records of life here at that time.

Plaque in the vestibule in memory of the Rev. T. W. Junk, erected by his son.

One thing, however, we do know that concerns our story. It arises out of the story of the Church of Ireland in Sixmilecross. The Parish Church, as I have told you, was in Carrickmore, an unfortunate placing, and most inconvenient for the people here. Probably some of them went to the Chapel of Ease at Clogherney, but even after this chapel became a parish church, it was no more central than Carrickmore. But shortly after the parish was divided, an attempt was made to get a church built in Sixmilecross, and to abandon the old church at Carrickmore. A vestry petition to the Primate stated that it would cost more to repair the old church than to build a new one, and that the late rector was willing to build a new church at his own cost in the townland of Sixmilecross. The change of site was not sanctioned by the Primate, but the church at Carrickmore was allowed to fall into ruin, and a church was built at Sixmilecross, but out of private funds. Our brethren here were thus in the same position as we were. To get a church of their own they had to build it themselves. It wasn't very well built. It had neither tower nor chancel, just four walls and a wooden roof. But it was stone-flagged, and had wooden pews, and so far was an improvement on our clay floor and turf sods. The people were no richer than we were, but the landlord was behind their venture, and that made the difference. That church was built on a good site, on the ground of the present Cross Row. It stood for about 50 years and was pulled down in 1811. The materials were sold. Mr. Hall bought the stone flags. The rector of Carrickmore bought the roof. We bought the walls, pulpit and pews for £9 10s.

Now there's something more in that sale than a mere account of what happened at an auction. It tells us that we needed stone and timber. What for? Obviously to repair in 1811 the church that we had built in 1786.

There's another thing we know about Mr. Brown's ministry. I made a light reference to it this morning. Our brethren of the Church of Ireland, after 1811, had no church

Andersons of the Cross

to go to except the new church at Carrickmore. They endured this for nearly 20 years, and they then seem to have resolved to put up with it no longer. They made a determined effort to get a church of their own, and in the meantime they asked the rector to arrange for regular services to be held in Sixmilecross. Our church was gladly placed at his disposal and for 5 years our brethren met here for divine service at 11 o'clock every Sunday morning. I never heard that it did us or the building any harm, and I recall with pleasure that these walls showed not the least sign of collapse when my old friend and school mate, the Rev. T. F. Campbell, came to our Sunday School examination, and examined our children in the Shorter Catechism. It was a new thing for them and a new thing for him, and maybe it was good for them both.

What else do we know about this period? We know that in 1833 the congregation numbered 796 men, women and children and that Mr. Brown's total salary was about £90 a year. Don't be too sorry for him. You can multiply that salary by 3. I'm not sure that you shouldn't multiply it by 4.

Mr. Brown was Clerk of the Upper Tyrone Presbytery and Dr. Latimer says that he was a very bad writer in the sense that his writing was very hard to read. His wife was long remembered as Madam Brown, and if tradition tells the truth, he hadn't more than got his breath again after a marriage till she had raided his pockets for the fee. When Mr. Brown died in 1851 he was the Father of the General Assembly.

He got leave to retire in 1836, and in that year a call was issued to the Rev. Matthew Clarke of Ballyhobridge. A large minority protested against the call, and the Presbytery asked for advice from the Synod whether or not Mr. Clarke should be allowed to accept it. The Synod said no. So that was that. Mr. Brown had to come back into service again for another 5 years. James McClean used to tell me of a vacancy here where the dispute between the two parties at the meeting to elect a

Plaque on the organ with the names of the members of the congregation who served in the Second World War 1939–45.

minister got so warm that they adjourned to the graveyard and had a pleasant continuation of the argument with their fists. I think it must have been on this occasion, for he also told me that the minister who got the call was supported by a large body of people who were of the same name as himself. That would fit in with this occasion, for the minister's name was Clarke, and the Clarkes were always numerous in this congregation.

Party feeling was high at this period, and the *"Belfast Newsletter"* of January 1824, reports a serious party fight in Beragh in which a young man named Smyth was killed, while the *"Enniskillen Chronicle"* reports what it calls a desperate party quarrel in Sixmilecross on the following Easter Monday. The paper says that fortunately there were no deaths, but there were many broken and bloody heads.

On the 5th of January, 1841, the Rev. Wm. Stuart Hazlett, who was a native of Newtownhamilton, was ordained in succession to Mr. Brown. The elders present at the ordination were Samuel Johnston, David Clements, A. J. Clarke and my great grandfather, Richard Forbes. Mr. Hazlett stayed here only two years. He accepted a call to Strabane and died two years later.

Meanwhile, a young man who was to live his life in Sixmilecross, and exercise a magnificent ministry here, was quietly preparing himself for his life-work. In 1838 the Monaghan Committee of the Synod of Ulster reported to the Synod that they had examined and passed Thomas William Junk, previous to his entrance to college. Mr. Junk was ordained on the first day of May, 1845. There were 120 families in the congregation and the stipend promised was £25. While Mr. Junk was still at college, the union of the two Synods, the Synod of Ulster and the Secession Synod, had taken place in 1840. Had that union not taken place, this church would have been deprived of one of its finest ministers, for this church was a Secession Church and Mr. Junk was a student of the Synod of Ulster.

Building Of Church

Mr. Junk wasted no time, for the year after he was ordained, this church in which we are worshipping today, was built. I will ask you to consider the formidable task to which this young minister and his people set themselves. The church cost £600. That was a tremendous sum. It would represent, at the very least over £2,000 of our money. And, it had to be raised, not merely in bad times, not merely in a season far worse than this season. It had to be raised at a time when famine stared the people plainly in the face. For the famine in 1847 was not only the result of wet weather and potato failure; it was equally the result of wet weather and potato failure in 1846. The mortar in the walls of this church was scarcely dry till the Relief Committees were at work in this very neighbourhood. On one single day, the 4th February, 1847, 116 people were admitted to Omagh workhouse. There were 1,300 people in the workhouse at the close of that day. There was a general reduction of rents in that year by landlords, and although the distress was nothing like what it was in the south and west, it was appallingly severe. Think then, think with admiration and astonishment of the courage and spirit of a minister and people in 1846, who built a church and, let me add, built it so well. Take a look at the walls outside and then at the porch that was built 54 years later, and you'll not be able to deny that the old work far surpasses the new.

Andersons of the Cross

Erection Of Manse

Mr. Junk and his people were not content with this venture. After some years they built a manse. 1879 was a bad year in which the potatoes rotted in the ground. Such seasons seem to have stirred the Sixmilecross people into fresh activity. If, in a season like that, they got the notion of a manse, and soon transformed the notion into a fact, may we not expect some fresh stirring in this year 1946, some new advance along the lines of 1846 and 1879 I trust you will think seriously of an advance of that kind.

The rear entrance to the National School on the Main Street where the Rev. W. F. Marshall received his early education. The schoolhouse was on the ground floor and the class rooms upstairs.

Photo courtesy of Marion Moffitt

I remember Mr. Junk as a venerable old man coming into the school with a little terrier dog. He was a fearless and faithful minister who preached the Word of Life here for 50 years. His preaching was animated and evangelical and, even in my time, there were still many of the older people to speak of him with admiration and respect. His services were long, as was the fashion of his time, and the Communion Service was rarely over before three o'clock. He was highly respected by his brethren in the Presbytery of which he was the Clerk. He passed to his reward on the 13th of April, 1899.

He was succeeded by the Rev. Samuel Dunn Stewart who was ordained on the 3rd December, 1895. Under his leadership, in a very short time, the church and manse were extensively repaired, new stables built and a field purchased to enlarge the graveyard — all this at a cost of £1,200. Mr. Stewart was a man of strong will, abundant energy and good powers of administration, and I am very sure that it was a man of his guts who was required at this period. For I recall clearly, although I was a small boy at the time, that there was more than a little opposition to these repairs, and a certain amount of fear that too much money was being spent and too much would have to be raised. We can bless his memory that he persisted and the Church Committee persisted, for the repairs made then, and their enduring nature are a perpetual monument to his ministry. After nearly 50 years they are still before your eyes, showing remarkably little sign of wear and tear. And no minister could have been kinder to a student member of his congregation than Mr. Stewart was to me.

Andersons of the Cross

Services In School

During these repairs the church was closed for eight months, and the services were held in the village school. And at this period also, the Rev. John Clarke, one of our own members, took charge of the congregation in the temporary absence of Mr. Stewart who was in America collecting funds. The first opening service was held on the 10th March, 1901 and was conducted by Professor Law Wilson. The services on the following Sunday were conducted by Professor Pettigrew. I distinctly remember being present at these services.

Mr. Stewart resigned on the 7th February, 1916 having accepted a call to Douglas Water Church in Scotland. I was installed here on the 20th April of that year. The rest of our congregational history is too recent to require examination. I resigned in April 1928 and there followed me successively, Mr.Bole, Mr. Eakin, Mr. Barbour and now Mr. Pattison.

I have no complete record of ministers who were reared in our membership, but I will mention the Rev. Archibald Armstrong, the Rev. James Love, the Rev. John Hutchinson, the Rev. John Clarke and the Rev. Herbert Clements. Over a century ago, there were two others in the Cousins family of whom I hope to learn further, so that the total as I know it at present would be mine.

And now I have reached the end of the story. It is by no means complete, but that is because I have been limited in time.

But there is something still to be said. There is no courtesy that a minister could show to one of his predecessors that your minister has not shown to me. It warms my heart to know that he is growing in influence and affection in this place. It warms my heart to be so sure that in his own quiet, modest way he will fulfil his ministry here with credit to himself and with blessing to you. He will be greatly encouraged by a generous response to the appeal which has been sent to your homes. I hope you will encourage him.

The Market House at the top of the Main Street (now demolished).

Bernisk Glen, Sixmilecross in June 1904.

Bernisk Glen

The sun's red rim
  Is hidden soon,
The low clouds dim
  The rising moon,
Shy badgers hide
  Still in their den,
But rabbits glide
  Through Bernisk Glen.

The twilight blurs
  Pool and moss,
No wind-breath stirs
  The withered grass,
Across the gap
  There's light to see,
A lone crow flap
  To attention.

Here all is still
  But for the vale,
Steals up the hill
  A farm-hand's hail,
A faint far clink
  Of can and tin,
Where lanterns work
  Down in Cloughfin.

Wee folk, they say
  Skipped to and fro,
Up Bernisk Way
  Long years ago,
But fairy ring
  And elf-shot cow,
And pixie king
  Are fool-talk now.

The greybeards rave
  Of highwaymen,
And of a cave
  In Bernisk Glen,
Of ghosts that wail
  Before the dawn,
But that's a tale
  Of years long gone.

Yet if you were
  In grey moonlight,
Alone up there
  Perhaps you might,
Just change your mind
  Like many men,
And look behind
  In Bernisk Glen.

Painting of W. F. Marshall by John Turner in 1959.

Andersons of the Cross

In the bog (May 1934) — Joe Anderson and Duncan Anderson (cousins) cutting turf.

Tea-time in the bog (May 1934) — Joe and Duncan having their afternoon tea.

Andersons of the Cross

Stack building in 1925 — the builder is Irwin Lewis, Edenderry. His helper is his nephew Charley Glenn

Sam McCausland, Laragh, Beragh cutting corn with a scythe in 1960.

Andersons of the Cross

Planting potatoes in the 1920s.

Inspecting cornstacks before introducing ferrets to tackle the rats, c.1920.

The ferret being introduced to the stack.

Armed waiting for the ferrets to deliver.

Andersons of the Cross

Tirooney Post office, Sixmilecross in 1930.

The Anderson boys who lived there in 1930 (l to r) Noel, Desmond and Ivan.

Sixmilecross L.O.L. on 12th July, 1967.

Back Row (l to r): Noel Anderson, Sam Kerr (holding banner), Basil Kerr, Crawford McCann, David Sloan, Brian Dixon, John Lyons, Robert Crawford, Roy Cobane, Ronnie Cobane, Jack Allen (holding banner).

Middle Row (l to r): Sam Bratton, Bill Jones, John Bratton, John Alcorn, Desmond Anderson, Myrtle Allen, William Kerr, Robin Lyons.

Front Row (l to r): Philip Adams, Irwin Anderson, Duncan Anderson, King Anderson.

Photography: Norman Anderson

235

CHAPTER 17

More Memories

Old Post Office and Academy, Omagh. Work on demolition commenced April 1939.

County Cinema, Omagh, erected on site of Old Post Office and opened on 13th January, 1940.

More Memories

Patricia and Gertie McCrory, daughters of the late Frank McCrory, at Ardmore in 1961. Patricia was receptionist to Leo McCloskey (dental surgeon) in Campsie Road in 1949.

(see poem on page 193)

McCloskey Family who resided at 17 Campsie Road, Omagh. c.1949. (l to r): John (dentist) wearing a Clongowes Wood blazer, Mrs. Amy McCloskey, Leo McCloskey (dentist). Front: Aideen and Neil.

Jack and the Beanstalk 1952

Eileen McCrory and Paddy McLoone.

Dickie Kennedy and Sheila Taggart.

Jack and the Beanstalk 1952

The Fairies

Back Row (l to r): Anne McBride, Rosa Murnaghan, Rosaleen Bennett.
Front Row (l to r): Winnie Curran, Anne Given, Helen Breslin, Mary McKernan, Monica McKernan.

The Chorus

Back Row (l to r): Margaret Mary Harris, Bernadette Phillips, Maura Donnelly, Bernadette McGuigan, Margaret McGuigan, Pearl Donnelly.
Front Row (l to r): Nan McCrory, Jean McDonald, Ellen Duddy, Carmel Gorman, Gladys McCann, Bernadette Drumm.

Commonwealth Day Youth Parade — Camowen Guides — John Street, 1959.

(l to r): Valerie Whitten (Standard Bearer), Lorna O'Neile, Olwyn Roy, Valerie Weir, Lynne Shorey, Jennifer Hart, —, Valerie Coote, Margaret Campbell, —, —, Eithne Todd.

Commonwealth Day Youth Parade— Omagh Cubs — John Street, 1959.

Back (from left): *Erville Millar, Dan Ferguson (R.U.C. Constable), Herbie McFarland, Mrs. Kathleen Twist, Jimmy McGinty, Carrickmore (Head of Dean Brian Maguire Secondary School), Bob McCormick, Sammy Moore (R.U.C. Constable) — all standing on footpath. Denzil Campbell, Keith Vance, Gary Brandon (top).*

Bottom (from left): *Robert Johnston, Neville Maguire, Clive Brandon, Raymond Hastings, Tom Potts, Anton Maguire, Keith Gilmore, Maurice Adams, Paul Watson, Robert Parke, Pat Mooney (Leader) (Kelso).*

Council — May 1967.

(l to r): Bob Henderson, James Eakin, Norman Wilson, William Coote, Harold McCauley, R. D. Glenny, Jim Charleton, Norman Anderson, J. P. Jameson, John McGale (Town Clerk), Tom McClay, Archie Burton, C. Walker, Stanley Wilson, Ira Love, Fred Charleton.

Omagh District Council Offices (entrance) on the occasion of a Ministerial Visit on 31st May, 1980.
Front Row (l to r): Councillors P. J. Bogan, B. M. P. Grant, Mr. Philip Goodhart (Minister D.O.E.).
Second Row (l to r): Councillors J. R. Hadden, J. B. Johnston, L. G. McQuaid, M. J. O'Hagan.
Third Row (l to r): Councillors A. C. McFarland, J. F. Skelton, E. R. McDowell.
Back Row (l to r): Councillors A. E. Barnett, B. J. Martin, H. M. McCauley, G. E. McEnhill, P. J. Donnelly.

Omagh and District Junior Chamber of Commerce Banquet — Monday, 24th May, 1965 — President: James Cunningham.
(l to r): *Raymond Beck, John McGale, Kevin Masterson, Harry Lynch, Frank Stewart, ——, Ronnie Hendly, John Aitken, J. P. Duff J.P. Norman Armstrong, Harold Wilson, Ennis McGuigan, George Stewart, Capt. Terence O'Neill, P.M., Mervyn Armstrong, Dai Waterson, Jimmy Cunningham, Cecil Grice, Brian Brennan, Dan McCurdy, Norman Wilson, ——, Peter Johnston, Eugene Scallon, Austin Lynch, Victor Leitch.*
Guests: *J. P. Duff,* J.P., *R. Parke, W. A. Colhoun,* J.P., *J. P. Robinson, J. S. Aitken, C. Grice, J. R. Landale,* C.I., *N. R. J. Wilson,* J.P., *J. McGale,* T.C., *His Grace The Duke Of Abercorn.*

Dunmullan Table Tennis Club — March 1988.

Back Row (l to r): Jimmy Smyth, Edmund Wiltshire (d), Canon J. Linnegan (d), David McFarland, Harry Beattie Jun., Iris Beattie (d), Marjorie Beattie, Eva McFarland, Ernie Buchanan.

Third Row (l to r): John Beattie, Daryll Torrens, James Beattie, Allison Kennedy, Nicola Kennedy, Pamela Baxter, Donna McFarland, Mavis Wiltshire.

Second Row (l to r): Howard Livingstone, Jonathan Marshall, Adrian Adams, David Robinson, Esther Robinson, Ruth Beattie, Richard Beattie, Emlyn Smyth, David Beattie, Andrew Craig, Stephen Pinkerton.

Front Row (l to r): Janice Pinkerton, Emma Smyth, Glenda McFarland, Sharon Beattie, David Marshall, Alan Pinkerton, Lynn McFarland, Joanna Craig, Elaine Smyth, Allison Beattie.

T.C. Autos, Omagh c.1968 (previously known as Colm Devlin's Garage). Acquired by Claude Maguire of Irvinestown on 31st October, 1971. The cars on the right of the garage are: Renault 16, Jensen Interceptor; Renault 4, Renault 8 and 10 (note the grill on rear engine, rear mounted), BMC 1100, Austin Mini, Metropolitan, Renault 4, BMC 1100, Renault 16, BMC Mini. Cars in front of pumps (from right): Renault 8 (rally prepared — note black bonnet and fog lights), Renault 4 Van (known as a Fourgon) and Triumph Herald. *Photo courtesy of Damien Maguire and named by Claude Maguire.*

Omagh Town

I remember dear old Omagh in those bygone days of yore,
I think of all those great wee shops, now many are no more;
There was Bertie Pollocks and also Tom McClays,
JBs down at the corner, now sadly they are all away.

It's great that Charlie Anderson's is still much to the fore,
Now it's been renovated, it's much larger than before;
There were Willie and Hughey, they were such gentlemen,
You couldn't but go in to them, your money for to spend,
Now the boss is Albert, William Martin's son,
He could sell you any hardware, from an eggcup to a gun.

Don't forget the Sweeteries, they belonged to Davy Young,
A very comic gentleman who was always having fun,
He also had a barber's shop and his barber had great skill,
No one could excel him, his name was Jack Somerville,
Jack often cut my hair and he did a tidy job
What do you think the cost then was, sure it was only just two bob.

Sam Steele, he sold bicycles and also Peter McAleer,
They called him Peter the Sloper, for his bikes were very dear,
But the reason for the extra cost — they had a three-speed gear.

Then there was that lovely building in the centre of the town,
It was the Royal Arms Hotel, but now they've pulled it down;
The tradesmen in those bygone days, their skill sure it was great,
Now when they erect a building it's all steel girders and concrete.

I remember going to Omagh on the 12th day of July,
The weather it was beautiful with a lovely clear blue sky,
We didn't take that long to get there as the horse was trotting hard,
And whenever we arrived we pulled into Porter's yard,
Then we hurried up the entry to get a decent view,
I remember it like yesterday . . it was 1932.

It wasn't like it was today as motor cars were very scarce,
But one thing you could rely on, was a ride in Pollock's hearse,
Harry Torney, he sold Hillmans, James Eakin, he sold Fords,
He would also sell you an Austin, if one you could afford,
Billy Charleton, he sold Vauxhalls and also Rovers too,
The Rovers they were very grand but they were very few.

If you were feeling hungry you could go to Willie Coote's,
Then up to Swan & Mitchell's to get yourself new boots,
Then if you felt like some refreshment after you got your tay,
You could go way up to Frank O'Kane's up on the courthouse brae.
There you could have a shanagh and there would be good fun,
The nice fellow who would serve you, his name was Eddie Quinn.

If you need a doctor, there was Dr. Mitchell and Barney Lagan too,
It wasn't like it is today, for doctors there were few,
Now we have Dr. Haldane, Dr. Fred's illustrious son,
The lovely books he has published, I have them every one,
They remind me of the good old days, to have them is a must,
Indeed they are a treasure, to me they're like gold dust.

I remember all my dear old friends to mention but a few,
Tom McClay, Fred Colhoun, Harry Torney, Captain Fyffe,
William Crawford and Dickie Wilton and also Tommy Strain,
Tommy was a memorable poet and his works they still remain,
Indeed, I was delighted when he got the M.B.E.,
And like my other old friends, his memory I hold dear.

Now to picture dear old Omagh, sure I have made a try,
I wish you all the best and now I'll say goodbye.

R. E. A. Marshall
(Doogary, 2004)

Omagh Golf Club — Committee 1960.
Standing (l to r): Frank McLaughlin, Cecil Maltby, F.R.C.S., Cyril Reilly, Maurice Bloomfield.
Seated (l to r): Sam Carlisle, Donal McGonigle (Club Captain), Arthur Simpson.

When the snow comes the Golf Club is taken over by the sleighs of the local children (1958).
(l to r); Valerie Whitten, Joan Clarke, Jayne McKeown, Richard Davison, Trevor Clarke, Gillian Davison.

Clubhouse

First Tee

Car Parks

Entrance

Greenkeepers' Shed

Dublin Road

Belvedere Park

Bottom Nine Holes
(across the Dublin Road)

Dublin Road Cemetery

Aerial view of the top nine holes in the early 1990s.

Omagh Model School 1949 (6th Class)

Back Row (l to r): Kenneth Graham, Robin Bell, Bertie Hemphill, Bobbie Kerr, Ronnie Barbour, Robin Mills, George Murdock.
Third Row (l to r): Hugh Thompson, Uel Henderson, Alan Turner, Wesley Allen, Dickie Liggett, John Burke, Brian Mclvor, Marcus Piggot.
Second Row (l to r): Ida Shortt, Kathleen Mclvor, Beth Adams, Bella Mills, Pearl Cockburn, Violet Semple, Frances Alexander, Florence Campbell, Myrtle Gault, Belle Kerr.
Front Row (l to r): ———, Carol McKibben, Joan Graham, Moira Colhoun, Dorothy McFarland, Muriel Campbell, Gladys Adams, Peggy Davison, Diana Braiden, Olive Braiden, Eileen Campbell.

Royal Mail Staff on duty on 18th February, 2006.

(l to r): John Baird, Jackie Rankin (Manager), Dominic McKenna, Pat O'Connor, Brenda Bradley, Andy McFarland (back), Brendan McCabe (front), Colin Paskin, Steven Kildea, Steven McCooey, (back), Paul Ballard (front), Kevin Flood, Terry Bonner, John McArdle, Paul Grimes, Alan McCombe, Kevin Bogle, Kenny McCain, Richard Donnell, Dan O'Neill, Leo Monk, Geoffrey Hawkes, Alan Spratt, Ian McGrath, Clare Campbell, Seamus Gormley, Albert McFarland, Mary Maguire, Jimmy Montague, Thomas Logue.   (Inset): Vauxhall Comber Mail Vans.

More Memories
BT Omagh Field Engineering

Some of the fleet of vehicles used to maintain the local telephone system.

Staff on 6th March, 2007.
Back Row (l to r): Jason Halcrow (Manager, Omagh Area), Shane Ward, Alan Donnell, Paddy Warnock, Noel Quinn, Ian Hamilton, Luke Deyzel.
Front Row (l to r): Pat Carlin, Dessie Friel, Davy Heaney.

South Pacific 1987 — *The first performance by the newly formed Omagh Light Operatic Society.*
Back Row (l to r): *Martin Donnelly, Dominic Kirwan, John Hession.*
Middle Row (l to r): *Eugene McFarland, Aishling Jennings, Louise Conaghan, Clare O'Neill, Malachy McCormack.*
Front Row (l to r): *Angus Mitchell, Godfrey Young, Sinead Martin, Jean Judge.* *Little boy at front: Gerard Batchelor.*

The Death of a Legend

Ben launching "Drink to the Bird" in Omagh Library on Tuesday, 8th October, 1991.

Carleton Summer School, Clogher (14th August, 1992).
Ben at Corrick House with his admirers from Omagh.
(l to r): Marie McGrath, Dr. Seamus Bradley, Anne Mulhern, Harry Kerr,
Moyra Teague, Anna Norton (Arthur Quinn in background).

Benedict Kiely 1919–2007

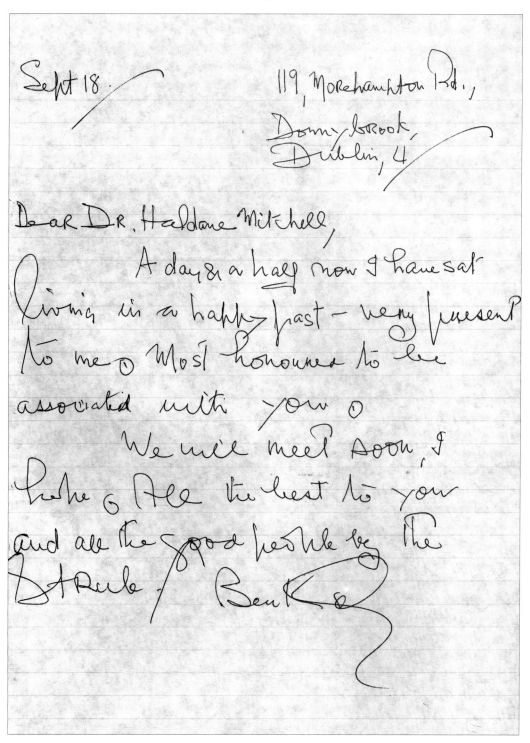

Sept 18.

119, Morehampton Rd.,
Donnybrook,
Dublin, 4

Dear Dr. Haldane Mitchell,

A day & a half now I have sat living in a happy past – very present to me. Most honoured to be associated with you.

We will meet soon, I hope. All the best to you and all the good people by the Strule.

Ben K

A letter received from Ben Kiely
after writing the Foreword to Volume 4 in March 1994.

INDEX